3984

Anti-Semitism:
The Road
to the Holocaust
and Beyond

Anti-Semitism: The Road to the Holocaust and Beyond

Charles Patterson

Walker and Company **New York**

First published in the United States of America
in 1982 by the Walker Publishing Company, Inc.

Published simultaneously in Canada by John Wiley
& Sons Canada, Limited, Rexdale, Ontario.

Book design by Laura Ferguson

ISBN: 0-8027-6470-3

Library of Congress Catalog Card Number: 82-8319

Printed in the United States of America

10 9 8 7 6 5 4 3 2 1

Library of Congress Cataloging in Publication Data

Patterson, Charles.
Anti-Semitism: the road to the holocaust and beyond.

Bibliography: p.
Includes index.
1. Antisemitism—History. 2. Holocaust, Jewish (1939-
1945) I. Title.
DS145.P36 1982   305.8′924   82-8319
ISBN 0-8027-6470-3   AACR2

To Gabriele

Contents

PART IV

Preface

THE PURPOSE OF THIS BOOK IS TO provide a useful introduction to a history of the anti-Semitism that led up to and beyond the Holocaust. The term "Holocaust"—which was first used widely in the 1960s to signify the Nazi destruction of European Jewry—suggests a sudden raging fire that bursts up out of nowhere.

But the anti-Semitism that erupted in Europe so violently did not start in 1939, or in 1933, or even in the modern era. It had ancient roots and a very long history. Long before the rise of Adolf Hitler, it had already poisoned the bloodstream of European civilization. What I have tried to do in this book is to trace the history of this anti-Semitism from its origins up to our own times.

My interest in this subject grew out of historical studies I undertook for my Ph.D. at Columbia, and out of religion and history courses I taught at the New School for Social Research in New York. Yuri Suhl, author of *They Fought Back: The Story of Jewish Resistance in Nazi Europe,* and Lucjan Dobroszycki of the YIVO Institute of Jewish Research in New York were helpful at key points early in the course of my research into the Holocaust.

I especially want to thank Dr. Gabriele Speier, to whom I have dedicated this book. She grew up in Germany and lived there for six years under the Nazis. Among the last to escape, she was also among the first to return—as part of the American medical team that entered the Dachau concentration camp in 1945 while the war was still being fought. I am grateful that she was willing to share with me her firsthand experiences of the Nazi era.

The many books and articles I have read are too numerous to list here, but the authors who proved to be the most helpful were Leon Poliakov, Lucy Dawidowicz, Edward Flannery, and Max Dimont. On the subject of anti-Semitism in the United States, I am greatly indebted to Nathan Belth's fine book, *A Promise to Keep: A Narrative of the American Encounter with Anti-Semitism*. About present-day anti-Semitism in other parts of the world I have relied on information from Isaac Alteras, Edouard Roditi, Richard Eder, Barbara Probst Solomon, Jacobo Timerman, W. D. Rubinstein, and the editors of *Encyclopaedia Judaica*.

Finally, special thanks go to my editor, David Sobel, for his patience and wise counsel.

C. P.

PART I

BABYLONIAN CAPTIVITY (587–538 B.C.)	**587 B.C.**	587 B.C. *Fall of Jerusalem; beginning of Babylonian captivity*
GREEK RULE OVER PALESTINE		333 B.C. *Alexander the Great establishes rule over Palestine*
		3rd Century B.C. *Early resentment against Jews of Alexandria*
		167–164 B.C. *Jewish revolt against Syrian emperor Antiochus Epiphanes*
ROMAN RULE OVER PALESTINE (Diaspora era begins)	**100 B.C.**	63 B.C. *Roman general Pompey captures Jerusalem*
		30 A.D. *Jesus put to death*
		66–70 *Jewish revolt against Roman rule ends with destruction of Jerusalem*
		c. 70–90 *Christian Gospels written*
	A.D. 100	132–135 *Second Jewish revolt against Roman rule*
		c. 395–400 *St. John Chrysostom denounces Jews of Antioch*
MIDDLE AGES	**1000**	1096 *First Crusade*
		1144 *First recorded "ritual murder" accusation*
	1200	1290 *Jews expelled from England*
		1306 *Jews expelled from France*
RENAISSANCE	**1500**	1492 *Jews driven out of Spain*
PROTESTANT REFORMATION		1648 *Decade of pogroms begins in Poland*
ENLIGHTENMENT		1654 *First Jews arrive in New Amsterdam (later New York)*

–1–
Ancient Roots

THE ROOTS OF ANTI-SEMITISM go back into ancient times when the religion of the Jews first began setting them off from their neighbors. While the other peoples of the ancient Near East worshipped many gods, the Jews (first called Hebrews, then Israelites) had only one god: an invisible deity who delivered them from Egyptian slavery, gave them their land, and created the laws by which they lived. So holy did the Jews regard their god that they made neither statues nor images of his likeness, nor did they utter his name.

Under the kings David and Solomon, ancient Israel was united and strong. Later, however, the land was divided into two kingdoms—Israel in the north and Judah in the south. When both were crushed by the invasions of powerful empires from the north, prophets blamed the disaster on the Jews themselves. They said that because the Jews had turned to other gods and had neglected their own ancient laws, their god had punished them. The ten tribes of the northern kingdom—now called the "lost tribes"—did not survive. However, the people of the southern kingdom did survive and came to be known as "Jews." Sent to Babylon as captives in 587 B.C. they were able to stick together and preserve their customs. They collected and preserved their sacred writings, honored their sabbath day, ate their food according to ancient practice, and circumcised their newly born males. By the time they were permitted to return to Jerusalem in 538 B.C. and to rebuild their temple, the religion that would carry them through the centuries—Judaism—had taken its basic shape.

Jews under the Greeks and Romans

IN THE FOURTH CENTURY B.C., Alexander the Great brought Greek customs to the East in the wake of his military conquests, challenging the Jews' distinctive way of life. The Greek civilization they encountered was impressive. It was a culture of sophisticated science, philosophy, poetry, history, and drama, and it attracted many Jews.

Many Jews left Judea to settle in the new cities the Greeks had established in the ancient Near East. In these cities, Jews participated in the social and commercial life, even though the requirements of their religion kept them apart from non-Jews. Alexandria, in Egypt, was the greatest of these Greek cities. It was founded by and named after Alexander himself in 332 B.C., and Jews settled there in large numbers. Within a couple of generations, Jews had learned the Greek language and needed to have their sacred writings written in Greek (for the first time, the Jewish "Bible" was translated into a foreign language).

The Jewish philosopher Philo (c. 20 B.C.–c. A.D. 50) even tried to join together the beliefs of Greek philosophy and Jewish scripture. In Jerusalem itself, upper-class Jews gave their sons Greek education and Greek names.

However, there were limits to the Jews' acceptance of Greek ways, for their strong religious traditions went back to David, Moses, and Abraham. The Syrian emperor Antiochus Epiphanes IV (ruled 175–163 B.C) even tried to stop them from practicing their religion. He forced the worship of the god Zeus Olympus upon the Jerusalem temple until the Jews revolted. Led by an old priest and his five sons, the revolt was successful. In 164 B.C., the Jews won the right to live by the law of Moses and regained control of the temple (celebrated yearly at the feast of Hanukkah).

From this religious revolt, the Jews went on to gain their political independence as well. Because of the decline of the Syrian empire, the Jews governed themselves for a century until the Romans took control of their land.

The Jews who continued to live in Alexandria were granted certain rights—to honor their sabbath and to refrain from participating in the city's religious observances (their religion prevented them from taking part in any ceremonies honoring other gods).

However, these privileges created tensions with the rest of the city's population. In fact, resentment against the Jews of Alexandria resulted in the first recorded anti-Jewish attacks.

Although the term "anti-Semitism"—which means "hostility toward Jews"—is only about a hundred years old, the prejudice it describes goes all the way back to Alexandria, where non-Jews resented Jews and the city's Greek writers attacked Jewish customs. In fact, one writer living around 300 B.C. challenged the claim of the Jews that they had escaped from slavery in Egypt. He wrote that they had in fact been expelled because they were lepers.

Apion was Alexandria's most prominent anti-Semitic writer. He lived in the third century B.C. and charged the Jews with every offense imaginable. He accused them of hating other people, and he claimed that they were traitorous because they wouldn't worship the gods of the city. He ridiculed their religious practices as well, saying that Jews rested on their sabbath day only because of injuries they sustained upon their expulsion from Egypt. He even accused them of killing human beings for religious reasons. He claimed that every year the Jews kidnapped a Greek, locked him up in their temple until he got fat, and then killed him as a religious sacrifice. Thus Apion became the first to accuse the Jews of *ritual murder,* a charge that was repeated often in later centuries.

These tensions between Jews and non-Jews continued under the Romans, who became the new masters of the eastern Mediterranean in the first century B.C. The special demands of Jewish monotheism clashed with the polytheistic practices of Rome and other cultures.* When the Romans granted Jews certain rights to practice their religion, resentment increased and Jews were labeled "clannish" and "hostile."

In Palestine (the area east of the Mediterranean where Israel now stands), friction between Jews and their Roman rulers reached crisis proportions in the first century A.D. The emperors sent officials called *procurators* to rule Judea directly. Religious Jews were especially upset by the presence of the pagan Romans in their midst. The tension exploded in A.D. 66 in a bloody war between Jews and Romans that ended four years later with the complete destruction of Jerusalem and its temple. Another Jewish revolt against Roman

---

Monotheism is the practice of worshipping only one god. Polytheists worship many gods.

rule flared up in the next century, but it, too, was harshly put down.

Roman writers continued the anti-Semitic attacks that had begun in Alexandria. Seneca called the Jews "that most wicked nation" and Cicero, Horace, Ovid, Martial, and Juvenal all joined in the criticism. Foremost among the Roman anti-Semites was the historian Tacitus. He called Jewish religious practices "rites contrary to those of all other men" and claimed that they were "sinister, shameful, and have survived only because of their perversity." Like most anti-Semites then and later, he did not seem to know very much about Judaism. He was certain that Jews worshipped donkeys, which they consecrated in their temples. He also criticized the Jews for "their obstinate solidarity, which contrasts with the implacable hatred they harbor toward the rest of men."

After the second Jewish revolt (A.D. 132–135) destroyed Jerusalem, it was rebuilt as a Roman city (called Aelia Capitalina). Jews were barred from their holy city. They could only approach as far as the outer wall of the temple.* The Roman emperor Hadrian even instituted a ban on circumcision. Jews were isolated more than ever just at the time when Judaism faced a serious threat from a new direction: the spread of Christianity.

Christianity and the Jews

IT IS IRONIC AND TRAGIC THAT Christianity, which began as a Jewish sect, should have grown up to become the most dangerous threat to Judaism. Jesus was a Jew, faithful to the law of Moses and the teachings of the prophets. He grew up and worked in Galilee, where Jewish patriotism was intense. He was steeped in Jewish scripture and the spirit of the *Pharisees,* the leading religious teachers of the time. People called him "Rabbi" and, like many religious Jews, he expected the imminent coming of the divine age, or the "Kingdom of God," as he called it.

However, like other religious, nationalistic Jews before and after him, Jesus (whose real Hebrew name was Jeshua) angered the Roman government because of his preaching, which was consid-

---

This wall, called the "Western Wall" or "Wailing Wall," still stands today in Jerusalem.

ered dangerous. On what turned out to be his final Passover trip to Jerusalem, Jesus was arrested and, upon the order of the Roman procurator, executed.

After the death of Jesus, his followers—most of whom had been simple fishermen and artisans—lived on in Galilee and Jerusalem. Called *Nazarenes* after Jesus's hometown of Nazareth, they continued to observe Jewish laws and to wait for the coming of the Kingdom of God, which Jesus had promised. In Jerusalem it was James, the brother of Jesus, who headed the Nazarenes for the next thirty years until he, too, was put to death in A.D. 62.

However, the future of Christianity did not remain long in the hands of these Aramaic-speaking Nazarenes. It passed on to an energetic, Greek-speaking Jew from Tarsus in Asia Minor by the name of Paul. He had never met Jesus and wasn't greatly impressed by the Nazarenes he did meet when he visited Jerusalem. What won him over to a belief that Jesus was the *Christos* (the Greek word for Messiah) was a vision. After his vision, Paul traveled all over the eastern Mediterranean preaching his own understanding of Christianity, which was rather different from the Nazarene version. Unlike the Nazarenes, who lived according to Jewish law in Jerusalem and Galilee, Paul took his message to gentiles as well as Jews. Through years of tireless work and extensive travel, he planted Christian congregations in Asia Minor and Greece.

However, the differences between Paul's teachings and those of the Nazarenes back in Jerusalem and Galilee soon became apparent. Not only did Paul preach to gentiles, but he also did not insist that these converts submit themselves to circumcision or to any of the other demands of Jewish law. The Nazarenes were outraged when they heard reports about Paul's negligence, and they summoned him to Jerusalem for an explanation. In Jerusalem, before the Nazarene elders, Paul acted as a devout Jew, observing all the details of Jewish law. However, he never changed his mind about the matter of his mission to the gentiles and his refusal to have these new converts treated like second-class citizens. In letters he wrote to his churches (now collected in the New Testament), he went so far as to claim that the law of Moses was no longer necessary, even for the Jews, and that Christ's teachings were sufficient. He also felt that everyone in the churches—Jews and gentiles, slaves and free persons—should be equal. When people from the Nazarene church in Jerusalem arrived at his churches to try to convince the gentile converts to obey the Jewish law, Paul denounced them as "Judaizers."

Paul did not think of himself as betraying the Jews. To the end of his life, he thought of them as the chosen people of God. He simply believed that the Christian mission should be aimed at gentiles as well and that he was specially chosen for that work.

The conflict between the Nazarenes and Paul that divided the early Christian movement was settled by a stroke of history itself. The fierce Jewish-Roman War (A.D. 66–70), which destroyed Jerusalem and its temple and killed so many Jews, also dealt a devastating blow to the Nazarenes, from which they never recovered. Whatever traditions and writings the Nazarenes possessed were lost or forgotten. Instead, Paul's churches survived and prevailed. Because of their attention to gentiles, these churches were the foundation for a Christianity that became separate from and even hostile to the Judaism out of which it emerged.

By the time the Christian gospels were written, in the latter part of the first century, Jews and Christians were separate, fiercely competitive groups arguing over whether or not Jesus was the Messiah-Christ promised in the Hebrew scriptures, and over which group—Jews or Christians—represented the "true Israel." Furthermore, by the end of the first century resentment and mistrust of Jews were widespread, due to their first revolt against Rome. The young Christian churches in the cities of the Roman Empire tried hard to distance themselves from their Jewish roots.

This desire for separation explains why, in the gospels written at this time, there was such hostility toward Jews, toward their religion, and particularly toward the Pharisees, who were the leaders of Judaism. The gospels tell the story of Jesus in such a way that it seems as if Jesus's real enemies were not gentiles, or even the Romans who put him to death, but rather the Jews—the Pharisees, the priests, and the Jewish people in general.

The first of the gospels to be written—The Gospel According to Mark—illustrates this anti-Jewish bias. It was written in Rome shortly after the end of the Jewish-Roman War (A.D. 70) when this resentment was especially strong. In Mark's gospel Jesus was persecuted at every turn by the Pharisees and priests of Judaism. In fact, this gospel claimed that the very first person to recognize the real worth of Jesus was not a Jew at all, but a Roman centurion present at his crucifixion who announced, "Truly this man was a son of God" (Mark 15:39).

Likewise, the Roman procurator who ordered Jesus's execution, Pontius Pilate, was pictured as someone who tried his best to be nice to Jesus. He tried to have Jesus released but was prevented from doing so by a mob of bloodthirsty Jews (the same people who cheered his entrance into the city several days earlier). In this way, the gospel puts the responsibility for the death of Jesus on the Jews, not on the Romans.

Matthew's gospel took this blaming of the Jews even one step further. There, Pilate's wife warns him to have nothing to do with wronging "that righteous man." Then, after the Jewish mob shouts for the death of Jesus (choosing to have the criminal Barabbas released instead), Pilate washes his hands in front of the crowd, saying "I am innocent of this man's blood." Here Matthew put into the mouths of the crowd words that were to condemn later generations of Jews: "And all the people answered, 'His blood be on us and on our children!' " (Matthew 27:25).

The gospels of Luke and John also painted Jews and Judaism as the forces that persecuted and drove Jesus to his death. Combined with the letters of Paul and others, the gospels form the sacred writings of the Christians—the New Testament. In this way, the anti-Jewish attitude resulting from the fierce competition between Christianity and Judaism in the first century became a permanent part of the Christian Bible and later Christian teaching and ritual. Many generations of later Christians grew up influenced by the negative picture of Jews painted in these scriptures, which Christianity considers to be sacred and infallible accounts of history.

Not surprisingly, this negative picture of Judaism and the Jews continued in the writings of the Church Fathers who wrote in the second, third, fourth, and fifth centuries and who gave Christianity its basic shape. The example of one writer, the fourth-century bishop of Antioch, John Chrysostom, suggests the tenor of their attitudes toward Jews. John Chrysostom was widely respected as a "Doctor of the Church" and was later canonized as a saint. In his sermons, however, he attacked the Jews of his city. He called them "lustful, rapacious, greedy, perfidious bandits . . . inveterate murderers, destroyers, men possessed by the devil." Their synagogue was a place of "shame and ridicule." Jewish religious rites were "criminal and impure." And why were the Jews so hateful? The answer, said the bishop, was in the gospels of the New Testament, which described how the Jews had killed Jesus. The Jews were hateful because of their "odious assassination of Christ."

–2–
Medieval and Early Modern Times

FROM THE FIFTH TO THE ELEVENTH centuries—the early "Middle Ages"—violence against the Jews was sporadic. In many places the relations between Christians and Jews were tolerable, even good.

In fact, in the eyes of some church leaders, relations between Christians and Jews were too good. One ninth-century archbishop complained:

> *Things have reached a stage where ignorant Christians claim that the Jews preach better than our priests . . . some Christians even celebrate the Sabbath with the Jews and violate the holy repose of Sunday. . . . They allow themselves to be plunged into such a sea of errors that they regard the Jews as the only people of God, and consider that they combine the observance of a pure religion and a truer faith than ours.*

The legal restrictions that church councils decreed during this period were designed to cut down on just such contacts. They were directed more against Judaism as a religion than against Jews as a people.

In 1096, however, with the advent of the First Crusade, an era of terror and massacre began for the Jews of Europe. Pope Urban II called for Christian armies to go to the Holy Land to free it from the control of the infidel (non-Christian) Turks. However, the vast throngs of knights, monks, and peasants who set out first turned their religious zeal on the Jews they met in northern France and along the Rhine River in Germany. Attacking the Jews who lived in their midst was perfectly logical to the Christian Crusaders. A French abbot asked, "What is the good of going to the end of the world, at great loss of men and money, to fight the Saracens, when we permit among us other infidels who are a thousand times more guilty toward Christ than the Mohammedans?" A German monk urged his followers, "First avenge the Crucified upon His enemies living here among us, and then go off to fight against the Turks!"

Along the Rhine, Crusaders massacred Jews in large numbers. Men, women, and children were put to the sword despite some efforts by local clergy and townspeople to protect them. In numerous cities along the Rhine and Danube Rivers, Jews were cut down by Crusader armies inspired by their mission to destroy the infidels.

Here is the eyewitness account of a Christian observer of what happened at Mainz in Germany:

> *Emicho and all his men, having taken counsel, proceeded at sunrise to attack the Jews with lances and axes. . . . Having broken the locks and knocked in the doors, they seized and killed seven hundred who vainly sought to defend themselves against forces far superior to their own; the women were also massacred, and the young children, whatever their sex, were put to the sword. . . . Only a small number of Jews escaped this cruel massacre, and a few accepted baptism, much more out of the fear of death than from love of the Christian faith.*

The First Crusade had a devastating effect on the Jews. As many as ten thousand were killed in 1096 alone—approximately one-third of the entire Jewish population of Germany and northern France. The massacres left surviving Jews shaken and dispirited. They became fearful and suspicious of the Christian world that surrounded them. They clung even more tenaciously to their faith. On the Christian side hostility against Jews increased, and the position of Jews in society became even more isolated. The Second Crusade fifty years later and the crusades that followed only resulted in more mob attacks on the Jews.

Resentment against Jews also increased because of the role some of them came to have in the economy. Prohibited from working the land, and excluded from Christian guilds, some Jews took up moneylending at the request of Christian princes. The Church forbade Christians from engaging in moneylending because of the belief that it endangered Christian souls. But since Christians regarded the souls of Jews as lost, it was left to them to provide this service, which was especially necessary due to the expanding commercial life of Europe. Caught in the middle between the princes who offered them some measure of protection and the general population, Jews were resented by both sides.

When powerful banking houses emerged in Italy and France, Jewish moneylenders were no longer essential. Jews were expelled from England in 1290 when the English king decided he did not require their services. Sixteen years later France expelled its Jews, and many German towns followed suit.

Jews were increasingly seen as homeless, wandering, and greedy enemies of Christ. They were often accused of poisoning Christian wells. They were suspected of maliciously causing any epidemic or mysterious death. When in 1347–1350 the Black Death devastated Europe, Jews were massacred by the thousands because it was rumored that they had somehow caused the pestilence.

Religious fervor during this Christian "Age of Faith" had a way of turning against the Jews. "Passion plays," which reenacted the story of the crucifixion for several days each year, spread the idea of Jews as "Christ-killers." Jews were also accused of desecrating the host (the wafer consecrated in the mass) when the Church decreed that the bread and wine used in the mass actually turned into the flesh and blood of Christ. Christians claimed that the Jews wanted to get possession of consecrated wafers so that they could stab, burn, and torture Christ's flesh to abuse him once more, as they had done at the original crucifixion. Many Jews were burned at the stake near Berlin in 1243 in the first recorded case of an alleged desecration of the host. Such charges and legally sanctioned murders continued well into the eighteenth century.

Jews were also accused of ritual murder, a charge begun by Apion that became widespread during the Middle Ages. The accusation claimed that Jews would capture and kill a Christian, preferably a child, for ritual purposes during Holy Week. The first case was reported in England in 1144 when the body of a young apprentice was discovered on Good Friday in the woods near Norwich. The rumor spread quickly that the boy had been murdered by Jews in mockery of the death of Christ. Riots followed and, although the charges were false, a local cult grew up around the relics of the dead boy. Similar accusations multiplied in Germany, France, and England, and persisted into modern times.

Christians attempted to convert Jews by persuasion and by force. The Talmud, the sacred book of Jewish tradition, was "put on trial" and publicly burned. Some Jewish people were forced to listen to lengthy sermons that were designed to win them over to the Christian faith. Beforehand their ears were inspected just in case they had plugged them up to ease the ordeal. In some places Jews had to wear special identification, such as a certain kind of hat, or a disc sown in the clothing.

Spain and Poland

IN SPAIN THE JEWS HAD PROSPERED under Muslim rule in the eleventh and twelfth centuries, but their position there declined when the Christians conquered the Moors. After this reconquest of Spain, so many Jews were converted through fear and coercion that these *conversos* ("converted")—whom the Spanish called *marranos* ("swine")—became a problem for Catholic Spain. In the eyes of the Church, these conversos were suspected of secretly practicing Judaism, or at least of following the Christian religion only halfheartedly. Furthermore, their presence in Spain was regarded by the clergy as a negative influence on the faith of Spanish Christians.

Popular resentment grew, and in the mid-fifteenth century violence broke out against Jews in various parts of Spain. In 1460 a Franciscan priest published an influential book attacking Jews— even those who were baptized—as a source of "bad blood" in Spain.

The Inquisition, a court appointed by the Pope, came to Spain to root out Christian heretics and marrano influence. In the unified Christian Spain of King Ferdinand and Queen Isabella, a Dominican by the name of Tomás de Torquemada was appointed Inquisitor General. Marranos by the thousands were burned at the stake and many thousands more were abused, imprisoned, and stripped of their property.

The fanatical Torquemada advocated the expulsion of all Jews from Spain, and in 1492 Ferdinand and Isabella finally ordered them all out under penalty of death. The thousands forced to flee had to endure extreme hardships in many lands, although those who went to Italy and Turkey were slightly more welcome. Those who went to Portugal had to face the Inquisition all over again. Some Portuguese Jews escaped across the ocean to Brazil. In fact, the very first Jews to arrive in North America were Portuguese Jews who left Brazil to settle in the Dutch colony of New Amsterdam (later New York) in 1654.

Only in Poland and Lithuania, where Jews went in large numbers, did they live in relative safety and prosperity. From the beginning of the Middle Ages, Poland became a refuge for Jews escaping the Crusades and various other persecutions in the German states. Later expulsions from the other countries of western Europe drove more Jews east into Poland, Lithuania, Galicia, and the Ukraine.

In Poland the nobility welcomed them and allowed them to establish themselves as a middle class of traders and government officials, between the nobles and the peasants. There they became relatively prosperous, developed their own distinctive culture and language (Yiddish), and formed a parliament that provided them with a measure of self-government they had not known since ancient times.

Then suddenly, in 1648, came perhaps the bloodiest decade in Jewish history up until that time. The Ukrainian cossacks, led by Bogdan Chmielnicki, rose up against their Polish overlords and ravaged Poland with a ferocious barbarism, reserving their worst cruelties for the Jews. In the ensuing chaos, Polish Jews were attacked from all sides—by the cossacks and by the cossacks' enemies. In all, seven hundred communities were destroyed, and Jewish deaths numbered somewhere from a hundred thousand to as many as five hundred thousand. The Jews of Poland never recovered. Many fled back to western Europe. Most lived on in poverty, consoled by little more than religious piety and messianic dreams. As a result of the partition of Poland by its larger neighbors at the end of the eighteenth century, the bulk of these Yiddish-speaking Jews came under the rule of the Russian czars.

The Age of the Ghetto

IN THE TOWNS AND CITIES OF medieval Europe, Jews tended to live in the "Jewish quarter," but by the sixteenth century such a quarter had become a walled ghetto under lock and key. Usually these ghettos—the most famous were in Frankfurt, Prague, Rome, and Venice—were located in the poorer sections of the city, and their gates were guarded by paid Christian gatekeepers. Sometimes restricted to a single street, these ghettos were overcrowded and confining. Because most employment was still closed to them, Jews were usually restricted to such trades as peddling, trading second-hand clothing, pawnbroking, and moneylending.

This enforced segregation strengthened Jewish solidarity and devotion to religious study, but it isolated Jews from the larger society and made them objects of ridicule. No longer feared as a mortal danger to Christian society, they were now portrayed in life and literature with demeaning images. Locked up behind the walls of ghettos, they were closed off from the immediate effects of the political, cultural, and religious changes of the sixteenth to the eighteenth centuries that brought Europe from the Middle Ages into the modern era.

The Christian humanism that emerged from the Renaissance at this time stimulated a fresh interest in the Hebrew Bible. However, even these humanists, who had the highest regard for Hebrew literature, persisted with their traditional prejudices. The famous Christian humanist Erasmus (1466–1536) said, "If it is Christian to hate Jews, then we are all good Christians."

The Protestant Reformation also had mixed consequences for Jews. Followers of the reformer John Calvin tended to view Jews favorably because they identified strongly with the ancient Jews of the Old Testament. The English Calvinists (called Puritans) who came to Massachusetts tried to model their society on the Old Testament and even gave serious thought to making Hebrew their national language.

But in Germany, Martin Luther (1483–1546) preached anti-Semitism to his followers. Early on, Luther had courted Jews, certain that once Christianity was purified of its corruption it would inevitably attract Jews. He even wrote a pamphlet—"Jesus Christ Was Born a Jew"—in which he defended Jews and urged a charitable attitude toward them.

The Jews, however, did not live up to Luther's plans for them, and he began attacking them ferociously. A few years before his death, he wrote "Concerning the Jews and Their Lies," and other attacks equalling those of St. John Chrysostom for their anti-Semitic virulence. With a new violence of language, he repeated all the old accusations against the Jews. They were, he said, ritual murderers, poisoners, usurers,* parasites, and corrupters of Christians. They were worse than devils and harder to convert than Satan himself. They were the anti-Christ doomed to hell. He advocated the destruction of their synagogues and the seizure of their books. He urged the rulers of Germany to take action against them, and in his last sermon he called for their expulsion from all the German states. Ironically, it was Luther who translated the Old Testament—the Bible of the Jews—from Hebrew into German for the benefit of future generations of Germans. Unfortunately, his harsh anti-Semitism was also a part of his legacy to the future of Germany.

Luther's attacks gave fresh impetus to anti-Jewish literature. With the recent invention of the printing press, books and pamphlets flooded Germany and other countries, accusing Jews of everything from secret crimes (including ritual murder) to sexual perversion.

A favorite target of anti-Semites was the Talmud. The biblical scholar Johann Eisenmenger combed through the Talmud to find every possible reference he could use to back up the old charges (and some new ones) against the Jews. After he died, his book *Judaism Unmasked* became a veritable bible for later generations of anti-Semites.

The Enlightenment

THE ENLIGHTENMENT—A PERIOD IN European history when reason, science, and the rights of man were emphasized—likewise brought ambiguous attitudes toward Jews. When the leaders of the Enlightenment—called *philosophes*—denounced the superstition and intolerance of the Christian Church, the Jews were often held up as examples of its worst victims. Important thinkers such as Charles Louis Montesquieu, Gotthold Lessing, and Jean Jacques Rousseau argued that Jews and Christians shared a common humanity and

---

Usury is the practice of lending money at illegal interest rates.

should therefore share equal rights as well. But when the philosophes praised Judaism, they did so mostly to criticize Christianity. They showed no great love of Jews as a people. They advised them to abandon their peculiar customs and to merge with the Christian majority.

Voltaire—perhaps the greatest of the philosophes—hated Jews. He was the sworn enemy of the Church and its superstitions, but he also detested Judaism and Jews. He wrote that Jews were the "enemies of mankind" and were fully deserving of all the persecutions and massacres that had come their way. He claimed that they were "most obtuse, cruel, and absurd," with a history that was "disgusting and abominable." In his *Dictionnaire philosophique* he concluded his entry on the Jews: "In short, we find in them only an ignorant and barbarous people, who have long united the most sordid avarice with the most detestable superstition and the most invincible hatred for every people by whom they are tolerated and enriched."

Nonetheless, the Enlightenment did help create an atmosphere that was to benefit the Jews. With the weakening of the power of the Christian Church over people's lives, a more tolerant attitude prevailed. The new emphasis on the "rights of man" advocated by the philosophes, and embodied in the American and French revolutions, was also helpful. It helped pave the way for the Jews to emerge from the ghetto to take their place as equals in European society.

PART II

FRENCH REVOLUTION	**1780**	1781 *Patent of Tolerance issued by Austrian emperor Joseph II*
AGE OF NAPOLEON		1791 *French Jews granted full citizenship*
	1850	1853 *Gobineau writes* Essay on the Inequality of the Human Race
		1858 *Baron Lionel de Rothschild admitted to English Parliament*
AMERICAN CIVIL WAR		1860 Alliance Israelite Universelle *formed*
		1862 *General Ulysses S. Grant orders expulsion of Jews from his Tennessee military district*
		1879 *Term "anti-Semitism" first used, by Wilhelm Marr*
	1880	1881 *Russian pogroms begin*
		1894–1906 *Dreyfus Affair in France*
		1896 *Theodor Herzl writes* The Jewish State
	1900	1905 Protocols of the Elders of Zion *published in Russia*
		1913 *Anti-Defamation League of B'nai B'rith established*
WORLD WAR I (Russian Revolution)		1915 *Leo Frank lynched*
		1917 *Balfour Declaration*
	1920	1920 Protocols *sells 120,000 copies in Germany*
		1920 *Henry Ford's newspaper begins anti-Semitic campaign*
		1921 *U.S. Congress drastically restricts immigration*

–3–
Emancipation

IN WESTERN EUROPE, THE AGE of the ghetto drew to a close in the late eighteenth and early nineteenth centuries. The Jews began emerging into the mainstream of society with the rights of citizenship. As long as Christianity had held sway over the life and thought of Europe, Jews had been at a decided disadvantage. However, as the Enlightenment's emphasis on rational thought took hold, the prospects improved for Jews wishing to enter more fully into the life of Europe.

This movement was aided by an improvement in the European economy that accompanied the end of the feudal order and the emergence of capitalism and the industrial revolution. With the end of the medieval ban on moneylending, the place of Jews in the economy came to be regarded with less hostility. Statesmen and capitalists alike regarded Jews with financial experience and commercial contacts across national borders as an economic asset. The general improvement in the lives of most Europeans meant that any Jewish accumulation of wealth did not stand out. The restrictions on Jewish trade and travel relaxed even before the political edicts officially freed the Jews from the confines of the ghettos.

Another important factor in the emancipation of the Jews was the willingness of the Jews themselves to absorb the ideas and values of the world beyond the ghetto. Such a change required them to loosen their adherence to ancient customs and religious practices.

There had always been individual European Jews—the philosopher Baruch Spinoza (1632–1677) was one—who had reached out to embrace and contribute to the thought of their time. But it was not until the eighteenth century that Jews in larger numbers began bridging the gap that separated the ghetto from the world that surrounded it.

The First Steps toward Emancipation

OFFICIAL POLITICAL EMANCIPATION FOR Jews began in 1781 when Joseph II (1741–1790) issued his Patent of Tolerance. It abolished special taxes on Jews and permitted them to leave the ghetto. They could take up any trade they wanted to pursue; they could open businesses and factories; they could enter Austrian schools and universities. The Patent also directed Hebrew schools to include in their studies the German language and the humanities.

Under the enlightened reign of Joseph II, "Salon Jews" made their appearance in Vienna. These educated, cultured Jews opened their drawing rooms to the aristocracy of Austrian society and the celebrities of music, painting, and scholarship. This contact with the Austrian upper classes was reserved for only a small circle of Jews who had ceased to practice their own religion. The great mass of Jews inside the Austrian Empire remained trapped by their poverty in the ghetto.

In Berlin, the capital of Protestant Prussia, there were also cultured and learned Jews who wanted to participate in German life and thought. Jews were first allowed to settle in Berlin during the reign of the Prussian king, Frederick William (1640–1688), and in 1712 they built and dedicated their first synagogue. They were few in number, but because they were oriented toward business and scholarship, they quickly became an integral part of Prussian life. As in Vienna, so too in Berlin there were Salon Jews who thrived in the world of German culture. Rebelling against the influence of the rabbis in the ghetto, a number of German Jews were baptized in order to complete their identification with and integration into German Christian society.

An emancipated Jew by the name of Moses Mendelssohn (1729–1786) did much to provide leadership to German Jews who were venturing beyond the ghetto walls. Born in the Dessau ghetto, he went to Berlin at the age of fourteen to receive a secular education. Caught up in the German Enlightenment, he became friends with the philosopher Immanuel Kant (1724–1804) and Germany's leading playwright, Gotthold Lessing (1729–1781). Lessing's play, *Nathan the Wise,* which was based on Mendelssohn's experience showed the Jew as a proud and dignified bearer of a rich tradition. The popular reception of the play throughout Europe did much to change the image of Jews that had built up during the age of the ghetto.

Mendelssohn was brilliant and was adored by the cultural world of Berlin. He was nicknamed the "German Socrates" because of his vast learning, his literary reviews, and his critical essays on art. More importantly for the Jews, he translated the Pentateuch (the first five books of the Bible) and the Psalms into clear, compelling German.

The translation was a breakthrough. It not only invited Jews to enter the world of German literature, but it invited educated Germans to regard the Bible as literature of the highest order. The translation offended *orthodox* Jews, but many young Germans cheered this dialogue between the two cultures and advocated a broadening of Jewish education. As a result, young Jews, guided by Mendelssohn's books and pamphlets, came into contact with western science, mathematics, literature, and philosophy. But in the process they remained Jews, albeit *reformed* Jews not bound by the dictates of ghetto authority.

Mendelssohn succeeded in winning the Prussian counselor of state, Wilhelm Dohm, over to the cause of Jewish emancipation. In 1781 Dohm wrote an important and influential book, *Concerning the Civic Amelioration of the Jews,* in which he accused Christian society of responsibility for the degraded condition of the Jews and argued strongly on behalf of their emancipation.

The French Revolution and Napoleon

THE MOST DRAMATIC MOVEMENT IN THE direction of Jewish emancipation took place in the wake of the French Revolution and the conquests of Napoleon that followed it. The Declaration of the Rights of Man in 1789 provided for religious freedom, but it did not mention Jews specifically. During the first two years of the revolution, Jews worked to secure their legal and civic rights. Delegations of Jews put their case before various assemblies of the revolution, and leading French statesmen took sides over the issue. Finally, in September 1791 a revolutionary assembly did grant the seventy thousand Jews of France full citizenship with equal rights and civic freedom.

Napoleon gave the cause of emancipation its greatest advance by means of his European conquests. One of his goals was to make all the Jews of France loyal Frenchmen. With dramatic flair, Napoleon called a National Assembly of Jewish Notables. He put twelve questions to the assembled Jews concerning their patriotism, marriage practices, and attitudes toward non-Jews. The notables succeeded in satisfying Napoleon with their answers and assured him that they would defend France to the death.

Napoleon then called a greater meeting of French Jews and called it the Great Sanhedrin, after the supreme council of Jews, which had not met since Roman times 1800 years earlier. Napoleon wanted the Jews to confirm their answers before this special body to make the promises binding on all Jews. The Jewish leaders had mixed feelings. They felt pressured, on the one hand, but they were also proud that this "Sanhedrin" would once again assemble. Jews around the world rejoiced and praised Napoleon.

This "French Sanhedrin" lasted only long enough to achieve Napoleon's desire of confirming the answers given by the Assembly of Notables. However, it also declared to the Jews of the world that their laws were religious, not secular, and that the authority of the rabbis did not extend into civil and judicial matters. This decree signalled an important change in the structure of Jewish communal life in Europe. During the Middle Ages, Jews had been a "state within a state," subject to their own religious and civil laws as interpreted by the rabbinate. Now they owed their allegiance to the modern countries in which they lived.

When Napoleon's armies carried the principles of the French Revolution into Holland, Belgium, Italy, and the rest of Europe, Jewish emancipation followed. Napoleon's liberation of Rome was an impressive show. By the light of burning torches, a French general read to a cheering crowd Napoleon's proclamation giving freedom, equality, and religious toleration to Italians and Jews. The

French destroyed the gates of the Jewish ghetto and made Pope Pius VI a prisoner of war. In Venice and other Italian cities the gates of the ghettos were burned down to symbolize the beginning of a new era. Italians linked arms with Jews and greeted rabbis as "Citizen Rabbi."

Reaction and the Continuing Struggle

AFTER THE FALL OF NAPOLEON, THERE was a reaction against Jews that accompanied the reaction against the liberal ideas of the French Revolution. Anti-Jewish agitation flared up in many places. In Germany, Prussia, and the Papal States (the Roman Church's land in central Italy where Pope Pius VII reestablished the ghetto), Jewish emancipation was undone. For the rest of the nineteenth century, the fate of the Jews was tied to the struggle for the cause of constitutionalism and reform. The revolutions of 1848 helped Jews win back their rights in France, Germany, Austria, and Hungary.

Freedom and democracy were thwarted time and again through the century, but in the end they prevailed in most European countries. The French revolted against the restoration of the monarchy, and the Greeks finally overthrew their Turkish overlords. Every blow against royal rule was advantageous to the Jews. As the Italians fought to gain their independence and achieve national unity, Jewish emancipation was won little by little. Sardinia granted equal rights to the Jews in 1848. Then the northern provinces, Sicily, Naples, and Venice, followed suit. Emancipation finally returned to Rome despite the relentless defense of the old order by Pope Pius IX. He maintained the ghetto and compulsory sermons until 1870, when the Papal States were finally captured by Italian armies.

The Jews of Prussia and Germany had had good reason to hail Napoleon as their liberator. Wherever the French ruled, the cause of Jewish emancipation advanced. The ghetto in Bonn fell in 1798, and one by one the other ghettos of the German states followed. However, Jewish advances were slower in Germany because the reaction against Jewish progress found many distinguished spokesmen. Several leading German thinkers and scholars were anti-Semitic as a matter of course, soon making Germany the center of

European anti-Semitism. Nonetheless, as Germany unified under Prussian leadership, Jews took their place in government, industry, finance, and the military, in spite of the prejudice. By the time Prussia fought against the French in 1870, there were over seven thousand Jews in the German army.

In England, where Jews had done relatively well and had long been prominent in English public life, equality was granted grudgingly. A bill to naturalize Jews, called the "Jew Bill," was proposed in Parliament over a period of many years and never enacted. The prime minister and leader of the Tory party, Benjamin Disraeli (1804–1881), was Jewish, but baptized. It was not until 1858 that full emancipation was achieved, with Baron Lionel de Rothschild seated in Parliament. Only then did the law begin to recognize the reality of the Jews' place in English life.

Economic Factors

THE EUROPEAN ECONOMY WAS ALSO AN important factor in the story of Jewish emancipation. The Jews who emerged from the ghettos entered a world caught up in the midst of a dynamic industrial revolution and benefited from the social and material advances that it brought in its wake. Seasoned by the generations of financial experience that had been virtually thrust upon them during the Middle Ages, many Jews successfully entered the fields of banking and commerce. Some rose to the top. The Rothschilds spread their banking operations throughout Europe, which led to the later charge that they were the leaders and financiers of a worldwide Jewish conspiracy.

The control Jews held over the money trade in the expanding economies of Europe was overestimated—deliberately—by anti-Semites. As traders and city dwellers, Jews were in the forefront of many commercial enterprises that grew out of the industrial revolution. However, there was no question of a conspiracy or even of a controlling interest. Writers critical of the rise of capitalism accused the Jews of being unproductive parasites on the economy. Many socialists took this point of view. Karl Marx, a Jew who had been baptized as an infant, accused Jews of being at the very core of the corrupt capitalism he so opposed.

The fact is that most Jews who emerged from the ghetto were not captains of finance at all but working people. Many joined and even organized guilds and unions, and a number of them, like Ferdinand Lassalle, Bruno Bauer, and Marx, assumed positions of leadership in the socialist and labor movements. When Marx radicalized socialist thought, many critics were prepared to call his movement "Jewish Marxism" or "Jewish radicalism."

Jewish emancipation turned out to be a mixed blessing. Full citizenship and access to trade, industry, and education did not give Jews equality in Europe. In fact, Jewish progress inflamed old animosities. Anti-Semitic fear and hatred festered, taking on a new "racial," rather than religious, shape. Jews were now resented simply for being Jews (changing religion did not help, as Jews who became Christians found out). The age of racial anti-Semitism was at hand.

–4–
Anti-Semitic Reactions

MUCH OF THE NATIONALISM AND anti-Semitism of modern German thought began as a reaction against the ideas of the Enlightenment and the French Revolution that spread across the German states in the wake of Napoleon's successful military campaigns. These ideas of revolution and equality were threatening to the rulers of the German states and principalities. Their discomfort with French influence, and with the emancipation of the Jews that came in its wake, turned into a fierce nationalism. Germans denounced the liberal ideals of the French—liberty, equality, and fraternity—and asserted the distinctiveness and superiority of the German *Volk* (people).

Racial Anti-Semitism

THE PHILOSOPHER JOHANN FICHTE (1762–1814) was the father of modern German anti-Semitism as well as German nationalism. According to him, the Germans were superior to the French, the Jews, and all the other peoples of the world. "Among all the modern peoples," he wrote, "it is you [the German people] in whom the seed of human perfection most decidedly lies." Only the Germans had a language that was pure, he claimed, and one day it would be the Germans who would usher in a new glorious era of history. In 1793 he argued against Jewish emancipation. The only way he could imagine giving Jews their rights would be "to cut off all their heads in one night, and to set new ones on their shoulders, which should contain not a single Jewish idea."

Other leading German philosophers and biblical scholars in the early part of the nineteenth century were also openly anti-Semitic. Georg Friedrich Hegel (1770–1831), who followed Fichte in the philosophy chair at the University of Berlin, glorified war, the power of the state, and German destiny in his lectures and writings. He predicted that one day Germany would have a powerful authoritarian, militaristic state that would rejuvenate the world. The great influence of Fichte, Hegel, and other German thinkers did much to set the tone and the direction of Germany's later anti-Semitism.

Anti-Semitism that was essentially racial in nature (Jews despised simply because they were descendants of Jews) became prominent in Germany in the 1870s. From there it sent waves out into France, Austria-Hungary, and even Russia, which had plenty of its own anti-Jewish hatred. After this outburst of racial anti-Semitism at the end of the century in Europe, it festered on into the twentieth century, the era in which it would be given its deadly ideological shape by the policies and programs of Nazi Germany.

In 1871 the anti-Semitic priest, Father August Rohling, published *The Talmud Jew,* a vicious attack on Judaism that went through many editions even after its refutation by respected scholars. The financial crash of 1873 increased the suspicion that somehow the Jews were responsible.

The very origin of the term "anti-Semitism" is German. It made its first appearance in 1879 in Wilhelm Marr's book, *The Victory of Judaism over Germanism,* in which he warned against the Jewish domination of German life. The distinction between "Aryan" and "Semitic" had originally applied to differences of language. Soon, however, racial theorists began making generalizations about the Aryan-Nordic race (represented in its purest form by the Germans) and the Semitic race (whose only representatives in Europe were the Jews).

In 1879—the year Marr's book was published—the German chancellor Bismarck turned against the National Liberal Party, some of whose leaders were Jewish. From that point on, anti-Semites openly attacked the role of Jews in the liberal democratic cause. In the *Reichstag* (the German Parliament), denunciations of Jews became commonplace.

Prominent in this upsurge of anti-Semitism was the Protestant court chaplain, Adolf Stöcker, who founded the Christian Social Workmen's Union to fight "Jewish Socialism" and the "Jewish domination of German life." A petition calling for restrictions against the Jews of Germany collected three hundred thousand signatures. Anti-Jewish boycotts were organized, anti-Semitic congresses were convened, and Jews were physically as well as verbally abused.

Jews were attacked from all sides because of their important place in the economy. On the one hand, they were accused of being greedy capitalists who controlled banks and department stores. On the other hand, when some Jews gained prominence in liberal and socialist circles, they were accused of being radicals and communists. Conservative Christians continued to perceive Jews as a threat to what was left of their social order. In the eyes of most Germans, the country's Jews—both emancipated Jews and those who had arrived more recently from eastern Europe—were regarded as an alien presence.

Two of the greatest men then living in Germany—the philosopher Nietzsche (1844-1900) and the composer Richard Wagner (1813-1883), whose operas glorified Germany's ancient myths and heroes—were both critical of Jewish influence. The attitude of many Germans was perhaps summed up by the respected historian Heinrich von Treitschke when he declared, "Even in circles of the most highly educated, among men who would reject with disgust any ideas of ecclesiastical intolerance or national arrogance, there resounds as if from one mouth: the Jews are our misfortune!"

Germany proved to be most receptive to the theories of Europe's two greatest apostles of racist thought. The first was Count de Gobineau, a French aristocrat who wrote the four-volume *Essay on the Inequality of the Human Race* (1853), which was received much more enthusiastically in Germany than it was in France, perhaps understandably so. He wrote that the Aryan race of northern and western Europe (most notably the Germans) was superior to all other races of the world. "The Aryan German," he declared, "is a powerful creature. Everything he thinks, says and does is thus of major importance." In his view, Jews were not only physically and morally inferior to Aryan Germans, but their very presence was a corrupting influence. Wagner helped popularize this Frenchman's views, and Gobineau societies sprang up all over Germany.

Even more influential were the ideas of Houston Stewart Chamberlain. He was an Englishman who moved to Germany, took up citizenship, married Richard Wagner's daughter, and wrote books in German glorifying the Germanic race, bringing him the admiration of Emperor William II, Adolf Hitler, and a host of other German readers.

Like Gobineau, Chamberlain found race to be the key to understanding history and civilization. His most influential book was *Foundations of the Nineteenth Century* (1899), in which he affirmed that the Germans were the most highly gifted of the world's races. The Jews, on the other hand, were a "negative" race, a people "lamentably lacking in true religion." He even went so far as to claim that Christ was not a Jew at all (long an embarrassment to anti-Semites) but an Aryan, which is why he became the god of the Germanic peoples. According to Chamberlain, the Germans had the right to be the master race because they had inherited the best qualities of the Greeks and Indo-Aryans. "God today builds on the Germans alone," he declared, "this is the knowledge, the certain truth, that has filled my soul for years."

Chamberlain became immensely popular in his adopted country and many have called him the "spiritual founder" of Nazi Germany. Although his twelve hundred-page book did not make for easy reading, over the years it was championed by many of the most educated Germans. The Nazis revered his memory, and by 1938, the sixth year of Nazi rule, his book had sold more than a quarter-million copies.

Before his death, Chamberlain did manage to meet the young Hitler at a time (1923) when most of Germany considered the fanatical ex-corporal something of a joke. But the old and ailing Chamberlain saw in him the new German Messiah. "You have mighty things to do," he wrote to Hitler the day after their meeting. "With one stroke you have transformed the state of my soul. That in the hour of her deepest need Germany gives birth to a Hitler proves her vitality. May God protect you!"

The lead of Gobineau and Chamberlain was followed by scores of lesser German writers, and in time assumptions about the superiority of the Aryan-German master race permeated popular thought. Inherent in this racist theory about the purity and destiny of the German people was also the assumption that Jews were impure, materialistic, corrupt, and dangerous.

Such assumptions spread from Germany to Austria-Hungary as well. In Hungary Jews were caught up in the middle of the struggle between the forces of conservatism and liberalism. Often they were hated by the minorities within the confederation—Czechs, Slovaks, Poles, Germans, and Hungarians themselves. In 1882 Jews were blamed for the failure of the "Christian" banking organization, *Union Générale*. The notorious Father Rohling was at the University of Prague attacking the "Talmud Jews" and trying to stir up ritual-murder accusations wherever he could. In 1882 there was a sensational ritual-murder trial in Hungary, which lasted over a year but finally collapsed when it was generally seen as the crude attack on Jews that it really was.

Austria was receptive to anti-Semitism, as the young Hitler who grew up there was to find out. Strongly anti-Semitic voices were increasingly heard. Restrictions were put on the role of Jews in commerce and in the universities. Ritual-murder charges were commonplace, and anti-Jewish disturbances were frequent. In the 1890s anti-Semitism was furthered by the appearance of several political parties, most notably the Christian Social Party under the direction of Karl Lüger, the mayor of Vienna. Lüger was a hero of the young Hitler, and during Lüger's long rule over Vienna, anti-Semitism remained open and virulent.

France: The Dreyfus Affair

IN FRANCE, THE BIRTHPLACE OF JEWISH emancipation, the anti-Semitic reaction to Jewish progress took hold more slowly than it did in Germany and Austria-Hungary. For one thing, there were fewer Jews. For another, most of them had lived in France for a long time and were very patriotic. Nonetheless, anti-Semitism lurked under the surface of French life.

In the 1880s, France was divided between the Third Republic— the liberal offspring of the great Revolution of 1789—and its conservative opponents. Generally, Jews were on the side of the Republic, grateful for their emancipation by the first Republic. On the conservative side, lined up against the Republic, were the royalists, who wanted the restoration of the monarchy; the Catholics, who resented the restrictions put on Church power; and the army. Each of these groups was sure that Jews were an alien power in their midst, bent on dominating French life and subverting its traditions. They regarded the Republic as a "Jew Republic."

The energies of French anti-Semites were united and strengthened by the publication in 1886 of Edouard Drumont's *La France juive*. Its two volumes held Jews responsible for most of the problems in French history and described them as especially dangerous because of their ambition to dominate French life and to control the state. This work reveals how different modern anti-Semitism had become from that of the Middle Ages. Then, the Jew had been depicted in the most negative terms (he was usually shown as hunch-backed and repulsive). However, the modern picture of the Jew showed him possessing superior intellect, learning, and skills, which he turned toward the conspiratorial goal of seizing control of the country.

Drawing on some of the older "Christian" arguments as well, Drumont's racist attack won an enormous following and made anti-Semitism an issue in the public debate between the Republic and its opponents. Drumont advanced his cause by writing several anti-Jewish pamphlets and by founding an anti-Semitic organization in 1889. He was also editor of the daily newspaper *La Libre Parole,* in whose pages he condemned Jews and their alleged defender, the Third Republic.

This movement was the background for the notorious Dreyfus affair, which held the French people's attention for over a decade and exposed their anti-Semitism to the world. In 1894 an army captain by the name of Alfred Dreyfus, the only Jewish member of the French General Staff, was accused of spying for the Germans. Behind closed doors he was tried, convicted, and sentenced to life imprisonment on Devil's Island. The principal evidence against him had been an unsigned letter, allegedly in his handwriting, but, as it turned out, a forgery.

For twelve long years, France became the center of an intense debate dividing the country. There were charges, countercharges, street fights, faked evidence, and retrials. There was also Emile Zola's dramatic letter in a Paris newspaper entitled *J'accuse* ("I

Accuse"), which helped unravel the army's conspiracy to hide the truth and protect the real culprit. It was not until 1906 that Dreyfus was exonerated of all charges by the French Supreme Court and finally set free. In the end, the anti-Semitic campaign failed, but anti-Semitism as a prevailing force in French life continued to live on.

The Origins of Zionism

THE DREYFUS AFFAIR HAD A PROFOUND impact on a young Jewish journalist named Theodor Herzl, who had been sent to Paris as a correspondent for a Viennese newspaper. Up to that time, he had been mostly known in Vienna for his plays and literary reviews. However, his exposure to the Dreyfus case and the vicious anti-Semitism that exploded around it jolted him into thinking more deeply about his Jewish identity and the plight of the European Jew. He concluded that Jewish assimilation into European society was impossible and that the only solution was for the Jews to have a national state of their own. This philosophy is known as Zionism. He outlined his ideas in *Der Judenstaat (The Jewish State),* which was published in 1896.

Herzl did not invent the idea of Zionism. The idea of the return of Jews to their ancestral home in a mystical, if not literal, way had long been a religious ideal. The ancient prophets of the Bible had envisioned a "return to Zion" (Zion was a high hill in Jerusalem). Around 1860, with the rise of modern European anti-Semitism, this religious concept began to be transformed into the more secular, political idea of an actual "return to Palestine." Some Jewish thinkers concluded that assimilation and emancipation were not the answers. Jews would never be secure or accepted merely by fleeing from one European country to another. Jews would only be safe if and when they could establish a country of their own.

After the publication of *The Jewish State,* Herzl threw himself into the task of making his Zionist ideas a reality. He called the first Zionist World Congress together in Basel, Switzerland, in 1897 and served as the organization's president until his death in 1904. At this historic first meeting, Herzl announced the goal of Zionism—"to create for the Jewish people a homeland in Palestine secured by public law." The meeting then went on to establish Zionist organizations in countries with large Jewish populations.

The first issue to divide the Zionist movement was whether or not Palestine was essential to the Jewish state. At the Zionist Congress in 1903, Herzl himself proposed that the Zionists abandon their hope of obtaining Palestine, then under Turkish rule, in favor of the British offer of a homeland for Jews in Uganda, Africa. When a majority of delegates refused to go along with that idea, Herzl joined the opposition in order not to divide the movement further, although some Zionists did leave because of this conflict. The Zionist goal was to buy land in Palestine from Arab and Turkish landowners for Jewish settlers. For this purpose, the Jewish National Fund was started.

Significant success was achieved in 1917 when Britain, then at war with the Turkish rulers of Palestine, issued the Balfour Declaration. It promised that the British government would help establish a national home for the Jewish people in Palestine. After the Allied victory in World War I and the establishment of the League of Nations, Britain was given a mandate over Palestine by the League, and Jews were then free to settle there. Colonization increased rapidly in the early years, but to please the Arabs the British later cut back and eventually tried to block Jewish immigration. This came at the very time when Jews fleeing Nazi rule were most in need of a refuge.

–5–

Persecution in Czarist Russia

THE SURGE OF ANTI-SEMITISM THAT originated in Germany and spread to Austria-Hungary and France affected Russia as well. Here this prejudice already had a long history. Under the blatantly anti-Jewish policy of the czars, the consequences of the new surge of anti-Semitism were even bloodier.

By the nineteenth century, over half the Jews in Europe lived in Russia, including those parts of Poland that Russia had annexed. There, the heavy Jewish populations were out of reach of the currents that had helped to emancipate the Jews of western Europe. The czars of Russia were suspicious of European ways.

Early Restrictions

JEWS WERE FORBIDDEN TO ENTER central Russia, but in the fifteenth century some Jews did appear in Moscow, where they attracted several converts. A Russian sect that copied Jewish practices grew up there. It included clergy, and even the head of the Moscow church. When the group was discovered, its members were tried by a church council and burned or imprisoned. The incident deepened Russian fears of Jewish influence.

However, with the expansion of Russia, an increasing number of Jews came under the control of the czarist government. In the seventeenth century, Russia acquired more Jewish subjects with the annexation of parts of Lithuania. In the eighteenth century, Jews who were living in what had been Swedish territory came under Russian rule. With the exception of Peter the Great, who allowed certain Jews to live in the provinces, the czars restricted the Jews. Catherine II (1729–1796; also called Catherine the Great) put all of Russia proper off limits to Jews. The three successive partitions of Poland put almost one million new Jews under Russian rule. Thus did Russia become the ruler of the largest body of Jews in the world.

Catherine the Great invited foreigners ("all except the Jews") into Central Russia, but Jews were allowed to settle only along Russia's western border, called the Pale of Settlement. There the Jews established their own self-government, which enabled them to maintain their language (Yiddish) and culture. However, for most Jews, the life was one of poverty and oppression with its burdens of governmental regulations and extra taxes. Some tried to make a livelihood in the countryside as merchants or innkeepers, but most were driven back into the cities by the hostility of the rural Russians.

Alexander I, Nicholas I, and Alexander II

THE CZARS OF THE NINETEENTH CENTURY decided that the best way to solve their "Jewish problem" was to "Russify" the Jews by weaning them from their reliance on the Talmudic instructions of their rabbis and from their role in the economy as middlemen.

When Alexander I came to the throne in 1801, Jews were allowed to pursue any occupations they desired; they were encouraged to shift to agriculture and handicrafts and away from trade and peddling. They were permitted to attend Russian schools and universities and were free to move from the Pale of Settlement into Moscow and other parts of Russia. As a result, a number of Jews shifted out of peddling into manufacturing and merchandising. Some became professionals and scholars. Although life in the villages (shtetls) continued to be difficult for most Jews, they tended to be slightly better off than the Russian peasants.

After the defeat of Napoleon and the Congress of Vienna, however, Alexander grew more conservative and fearful of the liberal ideas the French had spread across Europe. He embarked on a policy of herding all Jews back into the Pale away from central Russia. He died before his repressive policies against Russians and Jews alike could be fully implemented, but his brother Nicholas I, who ruled from 1825 to 1855, plunged the Jews of Russia into a dark night of persecution and repression.

Under his rule, Jews were expelled from their professions and driven back into the cities. A special conscription policy made Jewish boys of twelve to eighteen years of age subject to twenty-five years of military service. They were shipped off to the farthest outposts of the empire. Often their parents never saw them again. They either perished or were converted under pain of taunts or torture. Kidnappers prowled Jewish communities to abduct young Jews to fill military quotas.

In order to break the tradition of Jewish separatism, the government established schools for Jews that taught Russian language and secular subjects, in the hope that young Jews could be influenced to forsake their religious traditions. The program was favored by certain Jews, but it failed because of the resistance it met; the vast majority of Jews remained loyal to their traditional ways.

One edict formally dissolved Jewish self-government by putting Jews directly under Russian administration without the protection of Russian citizenship. The Jews immediately devised a new form of self-government by organizing "societies" for every conceivable activity and function. This allowed them to settle disputes among themselves without having to resort to Russian courts. Nonetheless, Jewish life had become increasingly difficult under Nicholas. By the middle of the century, the Pale where Jews were allowed to live had shrunk to half its original size, forcing most of the Jews there into a life on the edge of poverty and despair.

With the arrival on the throne of Alexander II in 1855, a new era of Russian liberalism began. Alexander freed forty million serfs, curbed the power of the Russian Orthodox Church, and reformed the government and the courts. Jewish hopes for a better life under his reign were fulfilled when he put an end to the conscription of young Jews, opened Russian schools to them, and ended the restriction to the Pale.

Alexander decided to use Jews to westernize Russia. He turned to the wealthier ones to help him develop Russia's industry. Because of the connections some Jews had with European banking houses, Alexander used them to help expand Russia's banking system. His policy of Russification (making Jews Russian) resulted in Jews entering the fields of law, medicine, banking, architecture, and industry, although the vast majority of them continued to live in the Pale, close to poverty. However, with the twenty-five-year conscription requirement gone and Russian schools open to them, hope spread through the Jewish community.

But as the years went by, Alexander's liberalism waned, and he grew resentful of Jewish involvement in the liberal and radical causes he had come to fear. The era of Jewish progress came to an end as some Jewish schools were shut down and restrictions on Jewish life were reimposed, including those on Jewish advancement in the military and in local government.

The growth of an intense Russian nationalism known as "Slavophilism"—with its slogan, "One Russia, one creed, one czar"—produced a new wave of repression and anti-Semitism. In 1867 a Jewish convert to Christianity by the name of Jacob Brafman charged that Jews were linked together in a conspiracy to seize control of the gentile world. The charge helped the government to justify its policy of reducing the strength and autonomy of the organizations that gave Russian Jews their solidarity. In this climate, several Jews were brought to trial on ritual-murder charges.

Pogroms

THE ASSASSINATION OF ALEXANDER II IN 1881 ushered in an even darker period for the Jews. Alexander III succeeded his father and came under the influence of Pobedonostsev, head of the governing body of the Russian church and a vicious anti-Semite. He saw Jews as instigators of radical and liberal movements and made them the chief target of his anti-revolutionary program. His decreed solution for the "Jewish problem" was "one third conversion, one third emigration, and one third starvation."

The first great *pogrom* (organized assault on Jewish communities) he arranged began on Easter 1881, striking hundreds of villages throughout southern Russia. While local authorities stood by and did nothing, Jews were murdered, maimed, and robbed. The governmental supervision of the attacks was obvious, because the attacks occurred almost simultaneously and followed the same general pattern everywhere. The government put the blame for the pogroms on Jewish "exploitation" of the peasants. The minister of state ordered an investigation—not of the pogroms, but of the "exploitation" that was the alleged cause. Despite protests in other countries, more pogroms took place before the end of the year, and the government instituted new measures against Jews.

In 1882 a vicious wave of pogroms swept over Russia with such force that finally the government was forced to stop them. Then it issued a whole new series of anti-Jewish edicts, narrowing the area of the Pale, forbidding leases and mortgages to Jews, prohibiting residence in villages, setting up educational quotas, and restricting their professional opportunities. These laws, originally meant to be "temporary," remained in force until 1914.

Under Nicholas II, who ruled from 1894 to 1917, the situation grew even worse. Viciously anti-Semitic, he reinstated a policy of pogroms and forced emigration. During these years under Alexander III and Nicholas II, Russian Jews embarked on a massive emigration that was the greatest exodus in Jewish history. They emigrated by the hundreds of thousands, mostly to the United States, which at that time still had unrestricted immigration. Between 1880 and 1910, two million Jews from the Russian Empire, including Poland and Rumania, entered the United States, and another half million came in the following decade, despite the disruption of the World War I years.

Nicholas met threats to his absolute rule with intensive repression and anti-Jewish measures. The minister of the interior stated publicly that he would drown the revolutionary movement in Jewish blood. In 1903 there was a massive pogrom at Kishinev that lasted for three days. Thousands of Jews were killed and many more were made homeless.

To combat the progressive forces of liberalism and constitutionalism, whose cause most Jews favored, the reactionary forces organized themselves into the "Black Hundreds." Their cry was "Down with the Constitution and with the Jews!" In 1905, in conjunction with the government, they instituted the most brutal series of pogroms in Russian history. During one week alone, hundreds of pogroms exploded upon Jewish communities all over Russia, leaving thousands killed, wounded, and homeless. Jews who could still manage to flee Russia did so, most going on to the United States or western Europe.

In the wake of the suppressed revolution of 1905, Jews were faced with more repression. New laws restricted them to the Pale, and in 1910 twelve hundred Jewish families were expelled from Kiev. Again the government restricted the number of Jewish students in institutions of higher learning.

The Beilis Trial and the Protocols of the Elders of Zion

THE EXTENT OF RUSSIAN ANTI-SEMITISM was revealed to the world in the Beilis "ritual murder" trial. In 1911 the mutilated body of a twelve-year-old boy was found in a cave outside Kiev. The evidence pointed to a gang of thieves, but pressure by anti-Semites channeled the investigation in the direction of Mendel Beilis, the Jewish superintendent of the brick kiln where a witness testified he had seen the boy playing on the day he disappeared. Beilis was arrested and sent to prison for two years. His trial drew international attention. The lamplighter who was the witness later confessed that he had been instructed by the secret police. The "expert" on ritual murder was a Catholic priest with a criminal record. At the trial, he was refuted by the rabbi of Moscow, who showed that the priest was ignorant of the Talmudic texts he cited as proof of the Jewish practice of ritual murder. Two respected Russian professors testified for the defense on behalf of Jewish values and against the traditional ritual-murder accusation. In the end, the Russian jury declared Beilis "not guilty." Fearful of revenge at the hands of anti-Semites, Beilis left Russia and eventually came to the United States. His story is the basis for Bernard Malamud's novel, *The Fixer,* published in 1966.

Russian anti-Semitism was also responsible for the greatest and most dangerous forgery of the twentieth century: the *Protocols of the Elders of Zion*. It was written in the last decade of the nineteenth century by an unknown author working for the Russian secret police in Paris. Fantasies about Jewish plots and conspiracies were as old as the charges of well-poisoning and plague-spreading leveled against Jews during the Middle Ages. The *Protocols* was an anonymous work based on an earlier French political pamphlet attributing ambitions of world domination to Napoleon III—but nowhere mentioning Jews or Judaism. The *Protocols* pretended to be a series of twenty-four lectures by so-called "elders" of Judaism about their secret plans to control and dominate the world. At this fabricated conference, these leaders of world Jewry discussed their plans to take over the government, the press, and the economies of various countries. They concluded that they already controlled a number of European states under the guise of modern democracy, and that they were well on their way to their goal of world domination.

Protocols was meant to influence the policy of Czar Nicholas II and to impress upon him the essential role of the Russian secret police in turning back this Jewish menace. Ironically, the intensely anti-Semitic Nicholas immediately recognized it as a forgery. Consequently the first Russian public edition of *Protocols,* which was published in 1905, did not arouse much interest.

The worldwide recognition of *Protocols* came after World War I when the war, the Russian Revolution of 1917, and the unrest in postwar Germany invited speculation about the hidden causes behind the turmoil. The text was circulated widely during the Russian civil war among the masses, in an attempt to turn them against the "Jewish Revolution." Undoubtedly it did much to contribute to the widespread pogroms in southern Russia between 1918 and 1920. Afterwards Russian émigrés publicized the *Protocols* in western Europe.

Beginning with its translation into German in 1919, *Protocols* spread throughout the Western world. Even though most intelligent people concluded *Protocols* was a forgery, anti-Semites went to great length to defend the authenticity of its picture of the Jews' secret plot for world domination. Its most receptive audience was in Germany. In Munich it came to the attention of the young Adolf Hitler. Once the Nazis came to power, they used it as part of their justification for war against the Jews of Europe.

In the United States, *Protocols* found a celebrated sponsor in Henry Ford, who took great pains to have it printed up in his weekly newspaper. It was also later printed and distributed in various Arab countries and the Soviet Union.

–6–
Anti-Semitism in the United States

JEWS WERE BUT ONE OF THE MANY European groups who came to the United States, and in the beginning their numbers were so small that they were barely noticeable. By the end of the colonial period, the Sephardic Jews (originally from Spain and Portugal) numbered no more than a couple thousand. In the middle of the nineteenth century, a larger wave of Jews arrived from Germany as part of a larger influx of German-speaking immigrants from Germany and central Europe. Only toward the end of the century did Jewish immigrants arrive from eastern Europe in great numbers as part of a still larger group of non-Jewish immigrants from eastern and southern Europe.

Mixed Reception

THE FIRST JEWS TO ARRIVE IN North America in 1654 were twenty-three Sephardic refugees from Recife, Brazil, where the Inquisition had arrived in the wake of the Portuguese capture of the colony. Peter Stuyvesant (1592-1672), the Dutch governor of New Amsterdam (later New York), tried to keep these Jews out of the colony (as well as Lutherans and Baptists), but he was overruled by his superiors in Holland. At that time, Holland was a haven for Jews fleeing the Inquisition, and there were Jews on the board of directors of the Dutch West India Company, which managed the colony. So the Jews were allowed to settle, and by 1657 they had acquired most of the rights of burghers in the colony, thus bringing to a close the first anti-Semitic incident in American history.

Elsewhere in the colonies Jews fared no worse than other religious groups who did not conform to the dominant church in each colony. In fact, there is no record of Jews being harmed physically for religious reasons. Most Protestant groups revered the Old Testament so much that they tended to look upon living "Hebrews" more with awe and curiosity than with hatred. Jews fared best in Rhode Island, where Roger Williams had established religious toleration, but they also settled successfully in New York, Pennsylvania, South Carolina, and Georgia.

In 1740 Jews in the colonies received a favorable boost from England. Parliament passed a law providing for the naturalization of all foreigners who had been resident in the colonies for seven years. Jews were also exempted from having to take a citizenship oath professing Christianity, although such oaths for high public office were still in effect. Jews also benefited greatly from the principles of religious freedom and the separation of church and state provided for in the United States Constitution.

With the increased immigration of German Jews in the middle of the nineteenth century, they became more conspicuous. From 1830 to 1880, the number of Jews in the United States rose from twenty thousand to three hundred thousand. Most came to escape the conservative reaction against Jewish emancipation and liberalism that followed the fall of Napoleon and the failure of the Revolution of 1848. While many settled in eastern cities, some migrated westward as traders. By the 1850s there were Jewish communities in Nashville, Cincinnati, Galveston, and St. Louis. The Gold Rush drew hundreds of Jews to San Francisco.

Resentment against Jews broke out openly during the Civil War. On December 17, 1862, General Ulysses Grant issued an order expelling "Jews as a class" from the Department of Tennessee, over which he ruled. The expulsion was to take place within twenty-four hours, and it was the most daring blow against Jews in American history. Grant accused the Jews of trading with the enemy. Upon hearing about the order, President Lincoln immediately canceled it. But the damage had been done. Jewish peddlers and traders around the country became the objects of anti-Semitic attacks that continued beyond the end of the war, as Jews, achieving business success and wealth, became ever more prominent in American life.

With success, American Jews encountered the barriers of social discrimination. Social anti-Semitism in America can be said to have started in 1877 when the Grand Union Hotel in Saratoga Springs, New York—the most famous resort in the country at the time—turned away the banker Joseph Seligman, the most renowned American Jew of his day. He had been a principal financial backer on the Union side of the Civil War, had been offered the post of secretary of the treasury in the Grant administration, and had been part of the Saratoga social scene for ten years.

However, when he and his family arrived at the Grand Union on June 13, 1877, he was refused accommodations. Because of the death of the owner, the hotel was now under the control of its executor, Judge Hilton. The hotel clerk informed Seligman that Judge Hilton "has given instructions that no Israelites shall be permitted in the future to stop at this hotel."

The Hilton-Seligman quarrel that ensued in the press was outspoken and bitter, and the anti-Semitism that erupted was blatant and ugly. Spokesmen of national stature—Mark Twain, Oliver Wendell Holmes, and the famous preacher Henry Ward Beecher—came out against Hilton, but anti-Semites spoke out boldly as well. No sooner did the dispute simmer down than another American leader stated publicly that he was going to exclude Jews, too. Austin Corbin, president of the Long Island Railroad, who was developing Coney Island as a fashionable resort, announced that "We do not like Jews as a class. . . . they make themselves offensive to the kind of people who principally patronize our road and hotel and I am satisfied we should be better off without than with their custom."

No legal barriers stood in the way of such discrimination. Rulings of the Supreme Court in the 1870s tended to support the trend toward social exclusion not only in the areas of recreation and leisure, but also in the broader areas of education, housing, commerce, work, and the professions. Such social discrimination became the way in which upwardly mobile Jews were excluded from social acceptance and from taking their rightful place in American society. At just about this time, when these patterns of exclusion were beginning to harden, a new, huge wave of Jewish immigration—the largest by far—arrived in America.

The repressive policies of Czars Alexander III and Nicholas II caused two and a half million Jews to emigrate from Russia to the United States between 1880 and 1920. Years of pogroms, persecutions, and unsuccessful revolution drove out approximately one-quarter of all Russian Jews. The influx of these Yiddish-speaking people overwhelmed the existing American Jewish community and only served to intensify the anti-Semitic feelings in American society. The anti-Semitism that non-Jewish immigrants brought with them from the Old World was added to the growing social hostilities and the earlier religious prejudice. But perhaps most significant of all was the racism of older Americans directed in general against the new immigrants from eastern and southern Europe. It was this bigotry that eventually succeeded in stemming the tide of immigrants—Jews and non-Jews alike—from eastern Europe.

Closing the Immigration Door

THE RACISM OF THE FRENCHMAN GOBINEAU, who viewed the Jews as a "mongrel race" and the superior Aryan race as the source of everything great and noble, found its way into American thought. In 1856, three years after its publication in France, his *Essay on the Inequality of the Human Race* was published in America, with a supplementary essay by Dr. Josiah Nott of Alabama. As a defender of slavery, Nott was a firm believer in the inequality of the races, concluding that superior and inferior races could not "live together on any other terms than that of master and slave."

Gobineau's racial ideas found an even more articulate and influential spokesman in Madison Grant, a New York socialite and anthropologist who founded the New York Zoological Society. He popularized Gobineau's ideas for an American audience in his *The Passing of the Great Race,* published in 1916. He argued that the more valuable racial stock of Aryan-Nordic origin which immigrated earlier from northern Europe—Anglo-Saxon and German— was being diluted by the influx of inferior stock from eastern and southern Europe: Poles, Italians, Greeks, and, of course, Jews.

In the great debate that led up to the restriction of new immigration, assumptions of racial superiority became commonplace in the thinking of many Americans. The move toward restriction began slowly enough. In 1882 Congress passed a law excluding from the country convicts, paupers, and mental defectives. Three years later, under pressure from organized labor, Congress passed a law prohibiting industry's recruitment of workers from Europe. In 1903 a law was passed to exclude anarchists, epileptics, and beggars.

With the debate over a literacy test law, the discussion became markedly more racial. Arguments were made in favor of the superiority of Aryan-Nordic immigrants (English, Germans, Swedes, etc.) who had come earlier over the "inferior" peoples (Jews among them) from southern and eastern Europe. In 1896, 1913, and 1915, Congress passed bills requiring literacy tests for new immigrants, but each time these were vetoed by the president. Finally, in 1917 a literacy test requirement was passed over the veto of President Wilson.

Senator Henry Cabot Lodge of Massachusetts wanted to make the law even more strict. He devised legislation that was aimed directly at Jews. He wanted the literacy test to be given in the language of the country from which the immigrant was coming, rather than in the language he spoke. Such a provision would have barred the immigration of Yiddish-speaking Jews of eastern Europe, who for the most part could not read or write Russian, Polish, or Rumanian. However, Lodge was not able to persuade the rest of Congress to go along with such a restriction.

In 1907 a commission to study the issue of immigration was formed. Four years later, on the basis of work conducted by a staff of three hundred at the cost of one million dollars, the Dillingham Immigration Commission (as it was called) published a forty-two-volume report with "scientific" evidence that the "old immigration" was superior to the "new." By giving official approval to the prevailing bias against the new immigrants, the commission paved the way for the adoption of the national origins quota system, which was enacted into law in the early 1920s.

To curb the flow of these "inferior" peoples, Congress passed the Emergency Quota Act in 1921, permitting only 3 percent of a nationality living in the United States in 1910 to be admitted into the country in any one year thereafter. In 1924 an even more restrictive law was passed. Under its provisions only 2 percent of any nationality residing in the country in 1890 were to be admitted each year. Since the proportion of eastern Europeans in the United States in 1890 was still relatively small, this law struck a severe blow to Jews and other people wishing to emigrate from southern and eastern Europe. In 1927 immigration was further reduced to an annual total of only 150,000. America's "open door," which had welcomed millions, was now barely ajar. For the Jews of eastern Europe who had not yet come, it was especially tragic, for within two decades they were to be engulfed by the Nazi nightmare.

The Leo Frank Case

THE DECADE FROM 1915 TO 1925 saw not only the adoption of the national origins quota system as a device to curb immigration; it also saw an alarming rise of anti-Semitism.

In 1915 a Jew by the name of Leo Frank was lynched in Georgia. Frank was born in Texas, raised in New York, and educated at Cornell. In 1907 he moved to Georgia to manage a pencil factory owned by his uncle. There he quickly established himself as a young businessman with a good reputation, married, and became active in community affairs. In 1913 he was elected president of the Atlanta Lodge of B'nai B'rith.

B'nai B'rith, a long-established Jewish organization, had recently started turning its attention to fighting the rising tide of anti-Semitism in America. It began a publicity campaign against the denigration of Jews in the public media—newspapers, books, films, plays, school texts, and so forth. In 1913 it launched the Anti-Defamation League. The League wrote to publishers of travel books whose ads read "No Jews Wanted," and it wrote to newspapers to protest objectionable references to Jews in news stories. Its efforts to curb the worst excesses of this prejudice in mass culture met with some modest successes.

However, no sooner did Leo Frank assume his position as president of the Atlanta Lodge than he received his shocking initiation into just how vicious anti-Semitism could be. In April 1913 he was arrested and charged with the rape and brutal murder in his factory of a fourteen-year-old girl by the name of Mary

Phagan. Jim Conley, a young black janitor at the factory, was also arrested. Named an accessory to the crime, he was sentenced to one year on a chain gang. On the basis of circumstantial evidence Frank, who had admitted seeing the girl and paying her wages to her on the day of the killing, was charged with murder.

The thirty-day trial began on July 28, 1913, in the midst of an unruly, menacing mob. One eyewitness recalled the atmosphere of the trial:

> *Mobs choked the area around the courthouse. Men with rifles stood at the open windows, some aimed at the jury, some aimed at the judge. Over and over, louder and louder the men repeated the chant "Hang the Jew, Hang the Jew."*

No deputies made any attempt to clear the windows or the courtroom. Nor was any attempt made to restrain the spectators from giving vent to their anti-Semitic taunts and insults.

Not surprisingly, the jury found Frank guilty, and the judge sentenced him to death. The case was appealed, but the State of Georgia Supreme Court upheld the verdict.

Throughout the twenty months of the trial and the subsequent appeals, a steady stream of anti-Semitic abuse poured forth, led in part by the racist politician Tom Watson, who had now added Jews to his hate list of blacks and Catholics. His periodical *The Jeffersonian* kept up a constant attack on Frank and on anyone who dared support him with "Jew money." Watson charged that such support was given "to free the convicted libertine." The paper went on to claim that the poor victim had been "pursued to a hideous death by this filthy, perverted Jew of New York."

Because Governor John Slaton of Georgia had serious doubts about Frank's guilt, three days before his term expired he commuted Frank's sentence to life imprisonment. Anticipating the reaction from the mob, Slaton had Frank moved from Atlanta to a better-protected prison farm. Troops were needed to protect Slaton and his family. So great did the hostility become that three days later when Slaton left office—Watson had denounced him as "King of the Jews"—he left the state entirely.

The frenzied atmosphere reached the prison, where one of the inmates slashed Frank's throat, wounding him severely. Four days later, a vigilante mob of about twenty-five men stormed the prison. They dragged the wounded Frank off to Marietta, where the girl had lived, and there they lynched him.*

The rest of the nation was shocked, but in Georgia Watson boasted: "A vigilante committee redeems Georgia and carries out the sentence of law. . . . Jew libertines take notice." Watson, who was elected to the United States Senate in 1920, found anti-Semitism to be a valuable tool in his rise to power. "It is a peculiar and portentous thing," he wrote, "that one race of men—and only one—should be able to convulse the world by a system of newspaper agitation and suppression, when a member of that race is convicted of a capital crime against another race." His anti-Semitism blended into the rising resentment against the new immigrants. "From all over the world," he warned, "the children of Israel are flocking to this country and plans are on foot to move them from Europe *en masse* . . . to empty upon our shores the very scum and dregs of the *Parasite* Race."

The Ku Klux Klan and Henry Ford

IN THE VERY SAME YEAR LEO FRANK was lynched, the Ku Klux Klan was resurrected. Under a burning cross on Stone Mountain, Georgia, the organization that had terrorized blacks throughout the South after the Civil War was reborn. Like the Klan of old, they wore hooded sheets and declared themselves to be protectors of white supremacy, but this time it was not only blacks they persecuted. Under the leadership of William Simmons, the Klan aspired to "unite white male persons, native born gentile citizens . . . who owe no allegiance of any nature to any foreign government, nation, institution, sect, ruler, or people." Opposition to Jews, Catholics, new immigrants, and "wets" (those against Prohibition) was added

* In early 1982, important information withheld for almost seventy years came to light. Alonzo Mann, who back in 1913 was a fourteen-year-old office boy at Frank's factory, confessed that he saw Conley carrying the limp body of the girl toward the basement, but because Conley threatened him he kept silent. Conley died in 1962, but Mr. Mann was glad to get the matter off his chest anyway. "I just hope it does some good," he said.

to the cause of white supremacy. "We exclude Jews," explained Simmons, "because they do not believe in the Christian religion."

The revived Klan started off slowly. From 1915 to 1920, it gathered a membership of only five thousand. However, once the Klan started using the new techniques of promotion and advertising, its membership expanded rapidly in both the North and the South. Frustration with modern life was one reason why many people with rural or small-town Protestant backgrounds were drawn to the Klan.

Almost overnight the Klan became a powerful force in national life. By 1924 its membership had reached between four and five million. They dominated the politics of many state governments, and they were present in large numbers at the 1924 Democratic Convention in New York City. In 1925 the Klan held a massive parade in Washington, D.C., down Pennsylvania Avenue past the White House.

In the wake of Klan influence came violence as well. Catholic churches were burned, and one Klansman who murdered a priest got off scot-free. The Klan claimed to favor law and justice but, more often than not, it encouraged vigilante justice. Between 1920 and 1925, there were 225 lynchings in the United States.

Jews were easy targets in a number of communities. The Klan backed boycotts of Jewish merchants, vandalism against their stores, and burning fiery crosses outside synagogues and other Jewish institutions. On "Klan Day" in October 1923, in Dallas, Texas, the new "Imperial Wizard" of the Klan told his audience of seventy-five thousand that Jews were not capable of attaining "the Anglo-Saxon level." "There is not a semblance of racial hate in my heart," he proclaimed, but continued, "Jews are an unblendable element . . . alien and unassimilable . . . mercenary-minded . . . money mad."

The Klan declined even more quickly than it had grown. Widespread publicity about its violence and organized opposition hastened its end. All three candidates in the presidential election of 1924 condemned the Klan publicly. For many, the last straw came in 1925 when the Klan leader in Indiana, who controlled the government of the state, was convicted of murdering a young secretary. Disillusioned members left the Klan in droves. By 1930 there were only nine thousand Klansmen left. In 1944 the Klan was formally disbanded, only to be revived again in the 1970s.

At about the same time, Jews were attacked from another direction. The famous automobile manufacturer, Henry Ford, launched his seven-year anti-Semitic campaign in the pages of his weekly newspaper, the *Dearborn Independent*. Beginning with the May 22, 1920, issue, under the direction of its editor and Ford's own secretary, the paper's war against the Jews was vicious and unrelenting. "When we get through with the Jews," Ford's secretary said in court once, "there won't be one of them who will dare raise his head in public." He went so far in his search for malicious gossip that he set up an investigative agency in New York to spy on the private lives of prominent Jews. Soon it became widely known that Ford's paper was in the market for anti-Semitic ammunition.

Not surprisingly the notorious anti-Semitic forgery, *Protocols of the Elders of Zion,* found its way into the *Independent,* where it was published in its entirety. The editor succeeded in improving on the text to the extent that anti-Semites now prefer to circulate the Ford version of *Protocols*. Using it and other material his paper collected, Ford also issued a pamphlet called *The International Jew*.

Ford seemed surprised by the reaction. The Anti-Defamation League and other Jewish groups strongly objected and circulated their own writings attacking the *Protocols*. When Ford continued his attacks, 116 distinguished Americans—including President Wilson, former presidents Taft and Roosevelt, Jane Addams, Clarence Darrow, and William Jennings Bryan—signed a statement defending Jews and denying the authenticity of the *Protocols*.

Ford's propaganda was finally suppressed by a lawsuit. When the *Independent* ran a series of articles accusing a Jewish businessman of trying to control the wheat market, he sued Ford for defamation of character. The case went to trial in Detroit, but Ford settled out of court.

In the meantime, Ford protested to the Jewish community that he had not been aware of the effects of his paper, and at the end of 1927 he stopped its publication. He even wrote to Germany to ask Theodore Fritsch to cease publication of the German edition of *International Jew*. By the advent of World War II, Ford seemed genuinely determined to dissociate himself from his earlier career of anti-Semitism, but by then it was too late.

PART III

CHRONOLOGY · Part III

		1889 *Birth of Adolf Hitler*
WORLD WAR I	**1920**	1920 *Hitler organizes Nazi Party program*
		1923 *Beer Hall Putsch*
		1925 *First volume of* Mein Kampf *published*
WORLD DEPRESSION	**1930**	1929 *Depression hits Germany*
		1933 *Hitler becomes German Chancellor; anti-Jewish legislation begins*
	1935	1935 *Nuremberg laws deprive German Jews of citizenship*
		1936 *Germany occupies Rhineland*
		1938 *Kristallnacht*
WORLD WAR II		1939 *German invasion of Poland begins WW II*
	1940	1940 *Germany invades Denmark, Norway, Holland, Belgium and France*
		1940 *Jewish ghettos created in Poland*
		1941 *Germany invades Russia*
		1941 *Death camps begin to be built in Poland*
		1942 *Wannsee Conference coordinates plans for "Final Solution"*
		1943 *Warsaw ghetto uprising*
		1944 *Deportation of Hungarian Jews to Auschwitz*
	1945	1945 *Germany surrenders*

−7−

Prelude to Disaster

AT THE HEART OF ANY DISCUSSION of anti-Semitism is the Holocaust: the extermination of six million European Jews in the midst of a war that killed millions of others as well. The Holocaust was not only the culmination of the anti-Semitism that had poisoned the bloodstream of European civilization for so many centuries, but it was also a mass murder of such unprecedented enormity that history can offer little by way of comparison to help us grasp its scope and meaning.

The most obvious causes of the Holocaust—German anti-Semitism and nationalism, Hitler, the Nazis, economic problems, and the humiliation and resentment felt by the recently defeated German people—began to congeal after World War I. That war and its aftermath had been especially hard on the Jews of Europe. Jewish civilians were vulnerable to anti-Semitic excesses on both sides, especially in eastern Europe, where the opposing armies swept across areas where the Jewish population was most thickly settled.

Nor in the East did the danger to Jewish communities cease with the end of the war. In Russia the civil war between the White and Red armies (1918–1920), which broke out after the Bolshevik Revolution, had a devastating impact on Jews, since each side regarded the Jews they encountered as sympathetic to the other side. The worst cruelty occurred at the hands of the White armies in the Ukraine, where the Jewish masses were considered agents of Bolshevism. It is estimated that sixty thousand Jews were killed in the conflict.

Likewise, the war between Soviet Russia and Poland in 1920, which swept across the Ukraine and the newly created state of Poland, subjected thousands of innocent Jews to anti-Semitic attacks. The fighting that broke out between Poles and Germans along Poland's western border right after the war also brought hardship on the Jews living in that area.

Postwar Germany

EVER SINCE THE DAYS OF NAPOLEON, anti-Semitism had been particularly fervent in Germany. With World War I, yet another wave of anti-Semitism swept the country. During the war itself, when things began to go badly—increased casualties, food shortages, no military victories to lift the morale—Jews became the scapegoats for these misfortunes. In the last two years of the war, anti-Semitic accusations reached a crescendo—it was claimed that Jews were shirking their duty and were profiting from the war.

Ironically, the Weimar Republic—which was created out of defeat and revolution after the war—gave Jews the complete equality they had been seeking for a century. Yet these Weimar years saw anti-Semitism active in all aspects of German life. Over four hundred anti-Semitic organizations and seven hundred anti-Semitic periodicals spread their message throughout Germany. Anti-Semitic bills were introduced frequently into the Reichstag (the German Parliament) and into the legislatures of the separate states. German young people, especially university students, were overwhelmingly anti-Semitic. The Free Corps war veterans used to march through the streets singing, "Mow down Walter Rathenau, the goddamned Jewish pig." Rathenau was the foreign minister in the Weimar government. In 1922 he was assassinated by German anti-Semitic nationalists.

Anti-Semitic propaganda was unrelenting. In 1920, the year after it was translated into German, *Protocols of the Elders of Zion* sold 120,000 copies. Jews were blamed for just about everything— Germany's defeat; the abdication of the emperor; the revolutions that took place after the war in Berlin and Munich; the economic problems of inflation; unemployment; and the depression that hit Germany in 1929. Frustrated Germans longed for a national unity and ancient purity, but instead they found themselves engulfed by a hostile urban, industrial world that many believed had been created and maintained by the Jews.

There were postwar anti-Semitic developments in other European countries, such as Austria, Hungary, Poland, and Rumania. Even in England and Belgium, anti-Semitic fascist organizations were formed (in 1932 and 1936, respectively). Yet in the face of all these harassments, Jews not only survived, but they also advanced the cause of their full emancipation and integration into European life. Nowhere were they more successful than in Germany itself.

The Jews of Germany

JEWS HAD LIVED ALONG THE Rhine River as far back as Roman times. They had not been expelled from Germany the way they had been from England, France, and Spain during the Middle Ages. But large numbers of them had fled east to the safer, more promising climate of Poland to escape the Crusades, the ritual-murder trials, the persecutions, and the uncertainty of life in the German states.

When the Jews of Prussia, Austria, and the other German states achieved their legal rights as full citizens, they went on to become the most assimilated group of Jews in Europe. Many left their Judaism completely behind, and some became practicing Christians. Many who did keep their religion practiced a more liberal form called Reform Judaism, which became popular in nineteenth-century Germany. Jews intermarried with German Christians and became strongly nationalistic. So assimilated into German society did these Jews become that after World War I some social scientists predicted that within two generations there would be no more Jews practicing their own religion.

The impact on Germany's life and thought of the country's Jews (who never comprised more than 1 percent of the population) was way out of proportion to their number. Their contributions to German progress and prestige were enormous. Three of the great intellectuals of the modern world were German or Austrian Jews: Karl Marx (politics), Sigmund Freud (psychoanalysis), and Albert Einstein (physics). Many others, like the composers Gustav Mahler and Felix Mendelssohn, were prominent in the arts. Of Germany's forty-four Nobel prize-winners before Hitler's time, eight were Jews and four were half Jewish. Thousands of Jews fought patriotically for Germany in World War I. Of the five hundred thousand Jews in Germany, one hundred thousand had served in the German military before the end of the war, over three-quarters of them fighting at the front.

Upon their emancipation, German Jews had turned to the "free professions," where guilds and associations could not exclude them. Hence, they were very well represented in the professions of medicine, law, journalism, education, research, the arts, and retail merchandising (a modern extension of the peddling they were forced to do during the Middle Ages). However, Jewish control of these professions was never as powerful as the anti-Semites liked to picture it.

As the Jewish integration into German life increased, anti-Semitism only became worse. The arrival in Germany and Austria of "eastern Jews" from Poland before and after World War I only complicated matters. They were not assimilated, and more often than not they proved to be an immense source of embarrassment to Germany's integrated Jews. The eastern Jews wore caftans and beards, spoke Yiddish, were poor, and usually worked as peddlers and sellers of used clothes. Some assimilated German Jews, as well as German anti-Semites, referred to these newcomers derisively as "yids" and "kikes."

But even assimilation or conversion did not protect Jews from suspicion, resentment, and ancient hatred. For centuries it had been argued that the "Jewish problem" would be solved when the Jews stopped acting like Jews and accepted Christianity as the "true faith." But even conversion did not win them acceptance, as many found out. In twentieth-century Germany, racial (rather than religious) anti-Semitism was becoming increasingly popular. The little people of Germany—the peasants, farmers, and small shopkeepers—looked jealously at the success and prosperity of these assimilated Jews and welcomed the racist ideas of anti-Semites.

Hitler and the Jews

ADOLF HITLER WAS BORN IN AUSTRIA on April 20, 1889, in the town of Braunau am Inn, close to the German border. Starting school at the age of six, he never stayed in one school for very long, since his restless father, a retired customs official, moved from village to village. When his father finally did settle down in the village of Leonding, he sent Adolf to high school in Linz. Adolf was a poor student and rebelled against his father's plans for him to enter the civil service.

After his father's death in 1903, when young Hitler was thirteen, he moved with his mother to an apartment on the outskirts of Linz. He dropped out of high school without ever graduating and lived at home with his mother, refusing to learn a trade or to get a job. Certain that he was destined for greater things, he dreamed of becoming an "artist."

During this time, he read everything he could get his hands on about German history and mythology. He loved everything German as intensely as he hated everything non-German. Although Hitler later claimed that he did not become a dedicated anti-Semite until he lived in Vienna, the one friend he seems to have had at this time recalled that in Linz Hitler was already avidly reading anti-Semitic literature and speaking against Jews, even though there were hardly any around.

Hitler applied to the Vienna Academy of Fine Arts two years in a row, and was rejected both times. When his mother died, Hitler set off for Vienna to spend what he later described as "the saddest period of my life" (1909–1913). Now completely alone—without parents or friends, without a trade or job prospects, without money, and without the admittance to art school he had wanted so badly—Hitler lived in poverty. He earned money only when he needed it by doing odd jobs or by selling his drawings. He started out living in a furnished room, but soon he was sleeping in flophouses and then in a run-down men's hostel. For his meals, he went to the city's charity soup kitchens.

For all his unhappiness, he looked back on these Vienna years as "especially fertile and valuable" because they gave him a chance to forge for himself "a world picture and a philosophy which became the granite foundation of all my acts."

During this time, his observations of the political unrest in Austria only hardened him in his hatred of Jews and the Slavic peoples who were agitating for their rights and national identities. He believed that the Germans were superior to all these peoples and that it was the Germans' historic mission to rule over them with an iron fist.

In Vienna Hitler's attitudes about Jews molded him into the

fanatically committed anti-Semite that he remained for the rest of his life. According to the long account of the emergence of his anti-Semitic ideas he gave in *Mein Kampf* ("My Struggle"), these ideas did not originate at home. While his father was alive, Hitler said he never heard the word "Jew" at home.

However, beginning about the age of fourteen or fifteen, he did start hearing the word with some frequency, either in political arguments or in discussions about religion. In fact, he said that he was not even aware there existed an organized opposition to Jews until he went to Vienna. In the Austrian capital of over two million people there were about two hundred thousand Jews, but Hitler said that in the beginning he took little notice of them.

At first he was embarrassed by the caustic tone of the city's anti-Semitic papers, but before long he was reading the nationalistic (and anti-Semitic) *Deutsches Volksblatt*. "I was not in agreement with the sharp anti-Semitic tone," remembered Hitler, "but from time to time I read arguments which gave me food for thought."

As Hitler came increasingly under the spell of the anti-Semitic Dr. Karl Lüger, whom he considered "the greatest German mayor of all times," he began to take special notice of the Jews.

> *Once, as I was strolling through the Inner City, I suddenly encountered an apparition in a black caftan and black hair locks. Is this a Jew? was my first thought.*
>
> *For, to be sure, they had not looked like that in Linz. I observed the man furtively and cautiously, but the longer I stared at this foreign face, scrutinizing feature for feature, the more my first question assumed a new form:*
> *Is this a German?*

As Hitler read the anti-Semitic literature that abounded in Vienna, his point of view about Jews took a more definitive shape. No longer did he regard Jews as Germans who merely had a special religion. Rather, he saw them as an alien and separate people. "Wherever I went, I began to see Jews, and the more I saw, the more sharply they became distinguished in my eyes from the rest of humanity." Even their physical appearance he found repugnant: "Later I often grew sick to my stomach from the smell of these caftan-wearers."

Hitler's anti-Semitism became even more intense when he saw Jews as responsible for what he called "all literary filth, artistic trash, and theatrical idiocy." He was certain they were behind the shocking aspects of Vienna's cultural and social life. "If you cut even cautiously into such an abscess, you found, like a maggot in a rotting body, often dazzled by a sudden light—a kike!" Hitler also became convinced that Jews were behind the city's prostitution and white-slave traffic. "When thus for the first time I recognized the Jew as the cold-hearted, shameless, and calculating director of this revolting vice traffic in the scum of the big city, a cold shudder ran down my back."

He went on to see Jews behind all the big liberal newspapers. "From the publisher down, they all were Jews," he wrote. He also saw them as being in control of the large socialist party (the Social Democrats) as well. He concluded that Jews were a dangerous foreign people who were trying to seduce the German soul with Marxist doctrines. They were a people whose secret mission was to undermine civilization itself. "If, with the help of his Marxist creed, the Jew is victorious over the other peoples of the earth," Hitler warned darkly, "his crown will be the funeral wreath of humanity and this planet will, as it did thousands of years ago, move through the ether devoid of men."

Nourished by the city's open anti-Semitism, Hitler's fixation on the Jews was well on its way to becoming the fanatical racial crusade of later years. "Gradually I began to hate them," he wrote. "For me this was the time of greatest spiritual upheaval I have ever gone through. I had ceased to be a weak-kneed cosmopolitan and became an anti-Semite."

In 1913 at the age of twenty-four, Hitler left Vienna for Munich, to live for the first time in the country he would one day rule. Some claimed later that he left Vienna at this time to avoid getting drafted into the Austrian army. However, the reasons Hitler gave in *Mein Kampf* were racial and show how fanatical his German nationalism had become:

> *I was repelled by the conglomeration of races which the capital showed me, repelled by this whole mixture of Czechs, Poles, Hungarians, Ruthenians, Serbs, and Croats, and everywhere the eternal mushroom of humanity—Jews, and more Jews. To me the*

giant city seemed the embodiment of racial desecration. . . . The longer I lived in this city the more my hatred grew for the foreign mixture of peoples which had begun to corrode this old site of German culture. . . . For all these reasons a longing rose stronger and stronger in me to go at least whither since my childhood secret desires and secret love had drawn me.

Nazi Anti-Semitism

HITLER WAS DEVASTATED BY GERMANY'S defeat in World War I. At the outset of the war, he had joined a Bavarian regiment and, except for the two times he was wounded, he spent the entire war at the front. He was a zealously dedicated soldier who never asked for a leave or complained about the war. Twice he was decorated for bravery, the last time in August 1918, when he was presented with Germany's highest award: the Iron Cross, First Class.

He was so involved in the cause of the war that sometimes he would startle the other soldiers by suddenly launching into angry denunciations of the enemy. The enemy he denounced were not the British or French soldiers they were fighting, but instead the "invisible enemies" at home in Germany, whom Hitler considered even more dangerous—the Marxists, pacifists and, of course, the Jews.

His hatred for these "enemies" on the home front had intensified when he passed through Berlin and Munich on the way back to the front after his hospitalization in the middle of the war. He saw "scoundrels and slackers" everywhere and, of course, he was sure they must all be Jews:

The offices were filled with Jews. Nearly every clerk was a Jew and nearly every Jew was a clerk. . . . In the year 1916-17 nearly the whole production was under the control of Jewish finance. . . . The Jew robbed the whole nation and pressed it beneath his domination. I saw with horror a catastrophe approaching.

The catastrophe arrived in November 1918 when Hitler was in a hospital outside Berlin recovering from temporary blindness caused during a British gas attack. In the hospital, he heard the news that Germany had lost the war. Hitler vowed to have revenge on those "November criminals" who had betrayed Germany, who had stabbed the Fatherland in the back. Hitler made his decision: "My own fate became known to me. I decided to go into politics."

In postwar Munich, Hitler got his start in politics when the Army assigned him to report on a tiny, obscure group called the German Workers' Party. When he discovered that they shared some of his ideas, he joined the party and very quickly urged them to organize bigger and bigger meetings.

At the beginning of 1920, Hitler organized a meeting in Munich's large and famous Hofbrauhaus where, in a thunderous speech, he outlined the twenty-five-point program of the Nazi Party. (Five weeks later, the party changed its name to the "National Socialist German Workers' Party" or, more simply, the "Nazis.") The program, which called for a bigger, greater, stronger Germany, wasted no time in showing its strongly anti-Semitic character. The fourth point made it clear that no Jews were wanted in the new Germany:

> *#4. None but members of the nation may be citizens of the State. None but those of German blood, whatever their creed, may be members of the nation. No Jew, therefore, may be a member of the nation.*

Furthermore, Jews were not to vote or hold public office (#6), they were not to own or even work on a German newspaper (#23), and any Jews who entered Germany after August 2, 1914, were to be expelled from the country (#8).

By the summer of 1921, Hitler was the undisputed leader of the Nazi Party. He personally directed the creation of the S.A. *(Sturmabteilung),* his private army of brown-shirted storm troopers, and designed the party flag with its swastika (hooked cross), connoting Aryan supremacy, authoritarian rule, and racial purity. Hitler explained the meaning of the flag this way: "In *red* we see the social idea of the movement, in *white* the nationalist idea, in the *swastika* the mission of the struggle for the victory of the Aryan man."

All the early Nazis were anti-Semitic. Hostility against Jews was so much at the center of Hitler's speeches and the party program that anyone with qualms about the party's extreme anti-Semitism would never have joined. Two of the first Nazi anti-Semites deserve special mention.

Julius Streicher, a sadistic bully from Nuremberg, was one of the most notorious Nazis ever to line up behind Hitler. He had organized his own "German Socialist Party" in Nuremberg and was, for a time, one of Hitler's rivals. However, when Hitler attempted to seize control of the Bavarian government in 1923, Streicher rushed to Munich to join him on his ill-fated march. In return, Hitler made him the Nazi boss of Franconia, whose center was Nuremberg. Called the "uncrowned king of Franconia," Streicher ruled his domain ruthlessly and capriciously. He carried around a large black whip, which he used at will, and no one in his territory was safe from prison or torture.

He achieved national fame with the publication of his viciously anti-Semitic weekly, *Der Stürmer,* which specialized in lurid and pornographic accounts of alleged Jewish sexual crimes and ritual murders. So obscene were its attacks that some other Nazis even found them embarrassing. But in the highly charged anti-Semitic atmosphere of Nazi Germany, his paper became a sensation. By 1935 it had achieved a circulation of eight hundred thousand.

The anti-Semitism of Alfred Rosenberg was of a higher, though no less deadly, order. He was a Baltic German raised in Estonia and educated at the University of Moscow, where he got his diploma in architecture in 1917. After the Russian Revolution, he came to Munich with a deep fear and hatred of Communists and Jews, whom he was certain were plotting an international conspiracy.

Rosenberg so impressed Hitler when they met that almost immediately Rosenberg became the "philosopher" of the Nazi movement. In 1923 Hitler put him in charge of the party newspaper, in whose pages he churned out endless editorials and articles on Nazi race theories. In his books, pamphlets, and speeches, Rosenberg expounded on Aryan supremacy, the purity of the German *Volk* (people), the "degenerate nature" of Jews, and the "poison" of Judaism. His theories found their fullest expression and widest distribution in his seven hundred-page book, *The Myth of the*

Twentieth Century, which sold half a million copies in Germany during the 1930s.

When the Nazis came to power, Rosenberg was first appointed to the foreign office, but then an office was created especially for him, putting him in charge of "Supervision of the Total Intellectual and Ideological Schooling and Education of the Nazi Party." After the German invasion of Russia in 1941, he was made Minister for the Eastern Occupied Territories. In that post, he became more personally involved in the Holocaust, which his writings had done so much to promote. He supervised the confiscation of Jewish property and the transportation of Jews to the death camps.

After the war, Rosenberg was tried and convicted at Nuremberg for his crimes against humanity. On October 16, 1946, he was taken to the gallows of the Nuremberg prison and there, along with Julius Streicher and eight other top Nazis, he was hanged.

The anti-Semitism of Hitler and the Nazis was expressed most fully in *Mein Kampf*. Hitler dictated the first volume of this book while he was in prison in 1924, following his failed attempt to seize control of the Bavarian government (later called the "Beer Hall Putsch"). He finished the second volume in 1926.

The book abounds with his intense German nationalism and his hatred of Marxism and democracy, but at its center is Germany's struggle with its mortal enemy—the Jews. Building on the thought of Chamberlain and earlier racists, Hitler regarded the Aryans as the master race. He believed that the maintenance of civilization depended on upholding the purity of the Aryan race. The enemy of this racial purity and "the mightiest counterpart to the Aryan" was the Jew. Hitler saw the Jews as having no culture of their own; he described them as parasites and bloodsuckers who merely lived off the achievements of others. Their religion was only a disguise behind which they concealed their evil designs. Wherever Jews existed, they contaminated art and culture, infiltrated the economy, undermined authority, and as "germ-carriers" poisoned the racial health of others. In short, concluded Hitler, the Jew "stops at nothing, and in his vileness he becomes so gigantic that no one need be surprised if among our people the personification of the devil as the symbol of all evil assumes the living shape of a Jew."

In the pages of *Mein Kampf,* the obsessiveness of Hitler's anti-Semitism is fully revealed. In it he describes a sexual nightmare of racial desecration: "With satanic joy in his face, the black-haired Jewish youth lurks in wait for the unsuspecting girl whom he defiles with his blood, thus stealing her from her people." He also drew on that older religious tradition of anti-Semitism that pictured Jews as Christ-killers and the enemies of Christianity.

Drawing on every type of European anti-Semitism available to him, Hitler took up Rosenberg's charge that behind the threat of Communism was a Jewish plot to dominate the world: "In Russian Bolshevism we must see the attempt undertaken by the Jews in the twentieth century to achieve world domination." Rosenberg's influence is also apparent in Hitler's use of the forged *Protocols of the Elders of Zion* as proof of a worldwide Jewish conspiracy. That a large and respected Frankfurt newspaper "moans" that the *Protocols* were based on a forgery ("the screaming of the Jewish press," Hitler called it) is "the best proof that they are authentic." Anyway, whatever the origin, Hitler goes on to say, the *Protocols* shows "the nature and activity of the Jewish people . . . as well as their ultimate final aims." Hitler wanted the book to be better known in Germany because "once this book has become the common property of a people, the Jewish menace may be considered broken."

Hitler felt that the battle against the Jews would have to be ruthless because nothing less than the racial soul of the German people was at stake: "The nationalization of our masses will succeed only when, aside from all the positive struggle for the soul of our people, their international poisoners are exterminated."

The means for this "extermination" may have already been in Hitler's mind. In the last chapter of *Mein Kampf,* discussing the subversive influence Marxist leaders had on the war effort, Hitler offered a possible solution to the problem:

> *If at the beginning of the War and during the War twelve or fifteen thousand of these Hebrew corrupters of the people had been held under poison gas, as happened to hundreds of thousands of our very best German workers in the field, the sacrifice of millions at the front would not have been in vain. On the contrary: twelve thousand scoundrels eliminated in time might have saved the lives of a million real Germans, valuable for the future.*

–8–

The Nazi Campaign against the Jews

AFTER THE DEPRESSION ENGULFED Germany and unemployment soared to six million, the Nazis were able to capitalize on the fear, resentment, and despair that gripped the nation. Blaming Jews and Marxists for Germany's troubles, Hitler launched his campaign to become a national leader. The rise of the Communists only played into his hands.

In 1930 the Nazis made their first dramatic showing at the polls. They collected 6.5 million votes and won 107 seats in the new Reichstag, where they did their best—along with the Communists—to undermine the government of the Weimar Republic.

The government went from crisis to crisis until finally, on January 30, 1933, President Paul von Hindenburg gave in to the inevitable. He summoned Hitler and made him the new head of state (chancellor), giving him the responsibility of forming a cabinet for a new government.

To strengthen his hand, Hitler immediately called for new elections, for which the Nazis prepared with massive demonstrations, radio propaganda, and strong-arm tactics. They even engineered the burning down of the Reichstag to convince the country that the Communists were planning a revolution that only the Nazis could stop. The total of seventeen million votes the Nazis did get was their highest yet, but it was far short of what Hitler needed to establish his dictatorship by a two-third vote of the Reichstag. He solved his problem by arresting all the Communist and some of the Social Democrat delegates.

On March 23, 1933, Hitler "legally" established his dictatorship. He had the Nazi-controlled Reichstag formally hand over its powers to his government. As one historian put it, "The street gangs had seized control of the resources of a great modern State, the gutter had come to power."

The Campaign Begins: 1933–1935

FROM THE BEGINNING, THE NAZIS HAD heaped abuse on the Jews through their speeches, their party program, their slogans, and their songs. A line in their party anthem, the Horst Wessel Song, ran, "When Jewish blood spurts from the knife, Then everything will be fine!"

Before the Nazis came to power, their violence against Jews had been confined primarily to random beatings and the desecration of cemeteries and synagogues. However, after January 30, 1933, Nazi storm troopers attacked Jews openly and vandalized their stores. In one city, Nazis went right into a court to beat up the judge and several of the lawyers, who were Jewish. The law was of little help. Hermann Göring, who was now in charge of the police in Prussia, said in a speech on March 11, "I refuse to make the police the guardians of Jewish department stores." So blatant was the violence that world opinion was aroused. In the United States, there was even talk of boycotting German goods.

After Hitler gained full control of the government, he turned his attention to what he regarded as the mortal enemy within the state: the Jews. On April 1, the Nazis set up a nationwide boycott of Jewish stores. All over Germany, the S.A. and the S.S. (*Schutzstaffel*—Hitler's elite black-shirted terror squad) stood in front of stores where they had painted "Jude"—the German word for Jew—on the doors and windows.

It did not last long; on April 4, Josef Goebbels, the Minister of Public Enlightenment and Propaganda, said that the boycott had been successful, and then announced that it was over. But the violence against Jews in public life continued. Judges and lawyers were beaten up, and local party officials put pressure on them to "retire." However, disorganized violence was not to be Hitler's policy. When Hindenburg objected that some of these harassed

Jews were war veterans, Hitler assured him that the solution to the Jewish problem "will be carried out legally, and not by capricious acts."

What followed was a flood of legislation directed at Germany's Jews (a total of four hundred anti-Jewish laws and decrees were passed by the Third Reich). The Nazis had long been planning their anti-Jewish legislation, but now that they were in power they were able to put into effect their "German" laws, based on race, as opposed to what they called the "Jewish-Roman" laws, which ignored racial differences. The very first of these laws—the "Law for the Restoration of the Professional Civil Service"—was decreed on April 7. It authorized what Nazi pressure had already begun to accomplish in cities all across Germany; it eliminated Jews and political opponents from the civil service and from the practice of law (as a gesture to Hindenburg, Jewish war veterans were exempted). Next, Jews were prohibited from being lay assessors, jurors, and doctors or dentists in state institutions.

On April 25, the "Law Against the Overcrowding of German Schools and Institutions of Higher Learning" limited Jewish attendance to 1.5 percent of the student body of schools and universities. But those who made the quota were not the fortunate ones. They were subjected to insults, isolation, and beatings, as German schools and universities fell increasingly under the control of fanatically racist teachers and administrators.

Further laws decreed that government officials couldn't hire non-Aryans and that Jews were to be excluded from all institutions of culture and entertainment (art, literature, theater, and film). The "National Press Law" ended the independence of newspapers and required that all journalists be Aryan.

As the volume and complexity of anti-Jewish legislation grew, Nazi racial and legal experts had to define what a "non-Aryan" was. All candidates for the civil service now had to provide proof of their "German blood." Most of the Jewish community had lived in Germany for centuries and were the most assimilated Jews of Europe, so that separating "Jewish blood" from "German blood" posed quite a challenge. On April 11, 1933, the Nazis decreed that a "non-Aryan" was any person "descended from non-Aryan, especially Jewish, parents or grandparents." Hence, to be "Aryan" in Nazi Germany, one had to have four grandparents all of "German blood." One Jewish grandparent (even if converted to Christianity) was enough to condemn one as "non-Aryan."

Other laws followed, designed to rid Germany of its "racial impurity." One canceled the naturalization of "undesirables"—eastern European Jews who had come to Germany during the Weimar Republic. Another made the inheritance of farms legal only for those who could show that they had no Jewish ancestry all the way back to 1800.

In their first six months in power, the Nazis succeeded in passing laws that excluded Jews from German public life—government, law, the arts, and the press. By the time 1933 was over, the Jews of Germany were in a state of fear and shock. Emigration increased (thirty-seven thousand Jews left the country that first year), suicides rose, and thousands lost their livelihood. They were reduced, in the words of one observer, to "despairing men, weeping women and terror-stricken children."

In 1935 Hitler moved more radically to separate Jews from Germans and to strip them of their citizenship. The "Law for the Protection of German Blood and German Honor" prohibited mixed marriages and any kind of sexual contact between Jews and Germans, a problem that had obsessed Hitler since his Vienna days. As added insurance against any further "mixing" of the races, the law prohibited Jews from hiring German women under the age of forty-five as domestic help in their households.

The "Reich Citizenship Law," also enacted on the occasion of the Nazi Party Congress held in Nuremberg in September 1935, fulfilled the goal of the fourth point of the party platform, which Hitler and the earliest Nazis had wanted as far back as 1920. The law took away the citizenship of the Jews; it made them "subjects" of the Reich rather than "citizens."

These so-called Nuremberg Laws marked the beginning of the end for German Jews. Jews were now set apart from Germans legally, socially, and politically. Now, as "subjects" of the Reich, they were put beyond the protection of the law, the courts, and the state. The first stage of the Nazi program was complete. The legal groundwork was laid for putting the Jews at the complete mercy of the state police, thus making them vulnerable to the harsher measures of economic exploitation, confiscation of property, and deportation that were to follow.

War Preparations and the Aryanization of Jewish Property

AS SOON AS HITLER HAD TAKEN control of the government in 1933, he had formed a secret National Defense Council to set Germany on a course of rearmament and military expansion. Six months later, Hitler gave the world its first clue about the direction his foreign policy would take; Germany withdrew from the League of Nations and pulled out of the international disarmament conference in Geneva.

Then in 1935 Hitler boldly announced that he would institute universal military service, create a German Air Force, expand the army to half a million men, and revive the German general staff—all in violation of the provisions of the Versailles Treaty. The Allies protested, but when Hitler said in a speech that all he wanted was "peace," both Britain and France believed him.

On March 7, 1936, he sent German troops marching into the demilitarized Rhineland, once again in flagrant violation of the Versailles Treaty. But the French army, at that time much stronger than the fledgling German army, did not oppose them.

That summer the Olympic Games were held in Berlin as if nothing unusual had happened. Not a single invited country protested Hitler's regime by not attending. The Nazis used the games for a huge propaganda display of the "New Germany." Their show was marred, however, by an embarrassing blow to the Nazi myth of "Aryan superiority." In full view of Adolf Hitler himself and other top Nazis, the American black athlete Jesse Owens won four gold medals. (Nazi racial theory took a similar blow two years later when the black American heavyweight champion Joe Louis revenged an earlier loss to the German boxer Max Schmeling by knocking him out in the first round!)

In that same summer, Hitler secretly launched his Four Year Plan, whose goal was to make the German economy self-sufficient and ready for the Nazi "holy war" against Bolshevik Russia where, in Hitler's view, "world Jewry" had secured its base for world conquest. Explicitly spelled out in the program was Hitler's plan to seize all the property of Germany's Jews when the war began.

That same year, he courted the Italian dictator Benito Mussolini and forged the Berlin-Rome-Tokyo Axis pact. He openly supported

Franco in Spain with supplies and personnel (including the Condor Legion of the German Air Force) against the Spanish Republic, which was supported by the Soviet Union. The "Jewish Bolshevist threat" was very much on Hitler's mind during this period. In his speech to the Nazi Party Congress at Nuremberg in September 1937, Hitler warned of an imminent world insurrection that "without doubt originates from the authorities of Jewish Bolshevism in Moscow."

By the time Hitler annexed Austria in the spring of 1938, the plight of the Jews in Germany had grown desperate. Stripped of their citizenship, their dignity, and in many cases their livelihood, a quarter of them—about 130,000—had fled by 1937. Tens of thousands of Jewish professionals, judges, civil servants, professors, teachers, actors, musicians, and journalists had been thrown out of their jobs. New decrees in 1938 prohibited Jewish doctors and lawyers from practicing their professions.

Many Jewish workers and employees were fired because of local Nazi pressure, while many small Jewish businesses fell victim to boycotts and street violence. But larger Jewish firms had fared better. Because these businesses brought in much needed foreign currency, there had been no official policy for their "Aryanization" (Nazi takeover).

In 1938, however, with military preparations in high gear and Göring firmly in charge of the economy, the Nazis made plans for the systematic confiscation of Jewish property. Three decrees were issued to speed up the process. They first made it illegal to "camouflage" the Jewish ownership of a business. Anyone guilty of doing so could be sent to a concentration camp. The second decree gave Jews two months to report the value of all their property abroad as well as in Germany. A portion of the statement hinted at the direction of these decrees: "The Plenipotentiary for the Four Year Plan (Göring) may take measures necessary to ensure that the use made of property subject to reporting will be in keeping with the interests of the German economy." The third decree defined a "Jewish" business: "A business enterprise is considered Jewish if its owner is a Jew." In the case of larger businesses and corporations, their "Jewish" character was determined by fixed percentages. However, to make sure the Nazis could legally steal as many businesses as possible, the decree declared a business Jewish "when it is under the dominant influence of Jews."

While these plans to remove the Jews from the economy were underway, plans were also being made to put Jews under tighter police surveillance. Jews were issued identification cards and the word "Jew" was stamped on their passports. To make it easier for the S.S. and the *Gestapo* (the German secret police) to keep track of them, all of Germany's Jews were required to assume "Jewish" names. Males were given the name "Israel," females "Sarah," and any other names Jews added to these had to be from an approved list of Jewish names provided by the Nazis.

The police state of Nazi Germany grew more and more menacing. Authorization to take someone into "protective custody" was extended beyond political opposition to include the offense of being simply "antisocial" or "undesirable." Jews were arrested and sent to concentration camps often on these vague grounds. The Four Year Plan called for every able-bodied person to work, and gradually the concentration camps became forced labor camps. They were the beginning of the Nazi slave labor system that grew so rapidly during the war as the Germans captured and enslaved millions of the people of conquered Europe.

The year 1938 was a good one for Hitler. In the spring he annexed Austria, and in the fall his armies occupied Czechoslovakia's Sudetenland. After a summer of threats against the Czech government for its alleged "persecutions" of Sudeten Germans, Hitler convinced the British and the French heads of government to come to Munich and agree to his seizure of the Sudetenland. Neville Chamberlain returned to London to assure the English people that the Munich conference had secured "peace in our time," but in fact it was simply the latest and the most transparent in a series of Allied capitulations to Hitler's threats.

In the wake of such Allied timidity, Hitler decided to strike out even harder against the Jews. A series of events that began on October 28, 1938, gave him that opportunity. On that day the Gestapo rounded up thousands of Polish Jews living in Germany and transported them back to Poland.

Earlier in the year, the Polish government had decided that Polish nationals living abroad needed a special stamp on their passports in order to retain their Polish citizenship. However, Polish consulates had instructions not to renew the passports of Jews who had been abroad for more than five years. Polish Jews who had been living in Germany for years found themselves stateless overnight. Heinrich Himmler, head of the S.S., reacted by ordering the immediate arrest and expulsion of all Polish Jews.

Thousands of men, women, and children were arrested all over Germany and Austria and were transported in boxcars to the Polish border. Since the Polish government didn't want them either, they had to survive there as best they could while the government decided what to do with them. During this difficult period, many of these Jews died. Only under pressure from abroad and from Jews and Polish liberals within the country did the government relent and allow them to enter.

Among the Polish Jews expelled was a couple by the name of Grynszpan, who had lived in Germany since 1914. Their son, Hershl, was a seventeen-year-old student living in Paris with his uncle. When he found out about what had happened to his parents, he bought a revolver, went to the German Embassy, and shot the third secretary of the embassy, Ernst vom Rath.

When Goebbels received the news of vom Rath's death early on the evening of November 9, he called for "spontaneous" demonstrations against the Jews. Hitler had told him that "the S.A. should be allowed to have a fling." That night a nationwide pogrom of terror, pillage, and murder descended on the German Jews. The local Nazi bosses and S.A. leaders were ordered to destroy Jewish shops, synagogues, and businesses. Reinhard Heydrich had informed the police all over the country that anti-Jewish demonstrations "were to be expected" and that they were not to interfere with these "spontaneous" demonstrations. Their job was to guard "German" life and property, especially against the spread of fires from Jewish to non-Jewish property. They were also to make sure foreigners were not molested (the Nazis didn't want any unfavorable publicity). The Nazis also issued instructions for the arrest and jailing of as many able-bodied male Jews as possible, especially rich ones.

That night the plate-glass windows of Jewish shops and businesses all over Germany were smashed, giving the night its name: *Kristallnacht* ("Night of Broken Glass"). The police watched as Jewish homes, businesses, and synagogues were burned to the ground, and in some cases the "night" lasted almost a week. In all, two hundred synagogues and over seven thousand Jewish businesses were destroyed. Nazi gangs entered Jewish homes and raped, plundered, and murdered at will. In the course of the week, it is believed that about a thousand Jews were killed, with thousands more beaten, bullied, and abused.

In compliance with Heydrich's instructions, about thirty thousand Jewish men were rounded up and sent to Germany's largest concentration camps: Dachau, Buchenwald, and Sachsenhausen. There they were subjected to sadistic torment. They were made to stand up outside all night and were then beaten and tortured during the day. For many Jews, this was the last straw after five and a half years of increasing degradation. So common were suicides that one camp broadcast this announcement: "Any Jew who wants to hang himself is asked please to put a piece of paper with his name in his mouth, so that we may know who he is."

Kristallnacht was a turning point for the Nazis. The intensification of their assault showed that they were not limited to the "legality" of their earlier anti-Jewish legislation; they would not hold themselves back from violence and brutality. It also made the Nazis surer of the German people. This direct and blatant frontal assault on the Jews created neither a storm of protest nor shocked horror. So indoctrinated and intimidated by the Nazis had the German people become that there were no demonstrations or complaints. Churches did not offer shelter to Jews, nor did Germans come to the aid of their beleaguered neighbors.

Kristallnacht provided just the excuse the Nazis needed to speed up their plans to strip the Jews of their property. On November 12, Göring held a large meeting of top government and party chiefs at which he said that the Führer wanted "the Jewish question to be now, once and for all, coordinated and solved one way or another." The idea was to involve all the agencies in measures "for the elimination of the Jew from the German economy."

The meeting produced further actions against the Jews. Jewish businesses could only be reopened when they came under non-Jewish management. Jewish children still in German schools were expelled. Jews were made subject to a curfew and barred from all public places—theaters, movies, beaches, parks, resorts, even sleeping cars on trains.

The meeting also produced two major decrees. The first, on

"Eliminating the Jews from German Economic Life," completed the removal of Jews from the economy; Jews were excluded from all retail stores, mail-order firms, from selling any goods or services, managing any businesses, or being members of a cooperative. The second, which was the brainchild of Göring, was a decree on "Penalty Payment by Jews Who Are German Subjects." It was a one-billion-mark* fine levied on the Jewish community for "the hostile attitude of Jewry toward the German Volk and Reich." That huge amount of money was to be used for the German war effort.

What to do with the Jews themselves, however, remained a problem. They were removed from the economy, stripped of their livelihoods, segregated from public and social life, removed from schools, shamed and humiliated, but they were still physically present. At the November 12 meeting, Heydrich had remarked that "the main problem, namely, to kick the Jew out of Germany, remains." At first Göring thought that ghettos might be the answer, but it was pointed out that such ghettos might become a shelter for criminals and a breeding ground for epidemics.

What to do with the Jews? It was a problem that would become more acute for the Nazis as German military successes during the early years of the war brought vast numbers of Jews under the control of the Third Reich.

Expelling the Jews

BY 1939 NAZI LEADERS WERE COMING to the conclusion that the best way to solve the "Jewish problem" in Germany was to force the Jews out of the country. It was Heydrich who set the example with his handling of the Jews in Austria.

After their seizure of Austria, the Nazis pounced on Austrian Jews. The S.S. terror that had been aimed at selected targets—labor leaders, socialists, communists, journalists, and other political opponents—was now directed at all Jews. Thousands of Jews were beaten and publicly abused. In front of jeering crowds, they were forced to clean the streets and public bathrooms. The Nazis sent

---

*A mark is a form of German currency. At the time, one billion marks was equivalent to over 400 million American dollars.

thousands more to German concentration camps and to the big new concentration camp they built in Austria—Mauthausen.

Under orders from Heydrich, Adolf Eichmann set up an office in Vienna to force the Jews out of Austria. By threats and terror, and by forcing Jewish leaders to provide information, Eichmann rid Austria of forty-five thousand Jews in six months. By the outbreak of the war, he expelled one hundred thousand more.

At the beginning of 1939, Heydrich was given the job of driving out those Jews remaining in Germany. A directive of January 24 established a Reich Central Office for Jewish Emigration to promote the "emigration" (expulsion) of Jews from Germany "by every possible means." The Nazis set up a Jewish organization to oversee this emigration and to supervise the life of the Jews left in Germany, now stripped of jobs and state welfare, their children barred from German schools.

Heydrich and his vast S.S.-Gestapo-state police network were put in charge of this organization and of everything else connected with Jewish emigration. Other Jewish matters were placed in Adolf Eichmann's Office of Jewish Affairs (given the code name IV-B-4). His job was to schedule, organize, and manage the expulsion of Jews from Germany, Austria, and now Czechoslovakia. The responsibilities of this job were to be magnified many times after the outbreak of war.

But where were the Jews to go? The rest of the world did not open its arms to them. Virulent anti-Semitism was affecting all of Europe. After all, it had been Poland's decision to keep its own Jews from returning that had doomed thousands of Polish Jews living in Germany and set in motion the tragic events of November 1938.

The League of Nations established a High Commissioner for Refugees from Germany, but the member nations were so unwilling to help that the new commissioner resigned in protest. In 1938 thirty-two nations met at Evian, France, to consider the problem, but the conference ended after a week when the countries showed that they would not change their immigration policies to help the Jews.

Jews who left Germany earlier in the 1930s had found refuge more easily, but by the end of the decade, when the need for refuge was even greater, countries all over the world closed their doors to the Jews. The United States admitted some Jewish refugees under its existing quotas, but it refused to change its immigration policy as the refugee crisis worsened.

Palestine would have been a logical place for Jews to go, but the British put severe restrictions on Jewish settlement in Palestine just at the time when it was most needed. The British had promised a "national homeland" for the Jews in their ancestral home but, in response to Arab pressures, they drastically reduced Jewish immigration to Palestine.

The tragic story of fleeing Jews with nowhere to go is illustrated by the ill-fated voyage of the ship *St. Louis*. It set sail from Hamburg, Germany, on May 13, 1939, with 937 Jewish refugees, all of whom had Cuban landing certificates. When they reached Havana, the Cuban government decided not to permit them to land. The ship, with its despairing passengers, was forced to cruise aimlessly while other governments, including the United States, turned down its plea for asylum. Only through the efforts of some Jewish leaders were the passengers on board the *St. Louis* finally admitted to England, France, Belgium, and Holland. Many of these were once more caught up in the Nazi nightmare when the German armies overran Europe a year later.

As the plight of Europe's Jews became even more desperate, there were other doomed voyages. The *Sturma*, a rickety cattle boat packed beyond capacity with 769 Rumanian Jews, set sail for Istanbul, Turkey, where the passengers hoped to get visas for Palestine. But the Turkish government would not let them land, and the British refused to let them go on to Palestine. The ship drifted for 74 days before it sank near Istanbul; all of its passengers drowned.

Hitler's plan for the Jews was taking a definite shape by 1939. In an important speech Hitler made to the Reichstag (now no more than a Nazi cheering section) on January 30—the sixth anniversary of his coming to power—Hitler turned to the subject that had obsessed him for so long: his personal crusade against the Jews. With unmistakable clarity, he uttered a chilling prophecy about the fate of Europe's Jews, to which he would refer time and time again during the war:

I have often been a prophet in my life and was generally laughed at. During my struggle for power, the Jews primarily received with laughter my prophecies that I would someday assume the leadership of the state and thereby of the entire Volk and then, among many other things, achieve a solution of the Jewish problem. I suppose that meanwhile the then resounding laughter of Jewry in Germany is now choking in their throats.

Today I will be a prophet again: If international finance Jewry within Europe and abroad should succeed once more in plunging the peoples into a world war, then the consequence will be not the Bolshevization of the world and therewith a victory of Jewry, but on the contrary, the destruction of the Jewish race in Europe.

–9–

German-Occupied Europe, 1939–1941

AFTER THE FALL OF CZECHOSLOVAKIA, Hitler turned on his next victim. On the morning of September 1, 1939, he unleashed his *Blitzkrieg* ("Lightning War") against Poland, and before the month was over the Nazis had crushed and occupied it.

Suddenly the Jews of Poland, Europe's largest and most vital Jewish community, were under Nazi domination, while the Jews in eastern Poland fell under Soviet control. The Nazis had set up "emigration" offices in Berlin, Vienna, and Prague to rid the Reich of its remaining Jews. Now, suddenly, the Nazis were overwhelmed with a dramatically enlarged "Jewish problem."

Eastern European Jews

UNLIKE THE JEWS OF WESTERN EUROPE, who spoke the languages of their adopted countries and had absorbed and contributed to Western values, the seven million Jews of eastern Europe had retained their own language (Yiddish) and culture, experiencing little assimilation or emancipation.

Because of brutal persecution by the czars, over two million Jews fled Russia between 1881 and 1918. Most of these came to the United States, but many also went to western Europe. Others went to Palestine and later became the founders and leaders of the state of Israel. Even more might have left, but most were desperately poor. Thousands of these Jews lived in shtetls, where they eked out a living trading goods and services with the illiterate peasants of the countryside. However, Jews were well represented in the larger cities as well. Some of these urban Jews—especially those who succeeded in middle-class occupations—adopted the ways of their gentile neighbors, but such assimilation in the east was limited—and certainly not as pervasive as in the west.

In spite of all this poverty and czarist repression, the Jews did preserve and maintain their language, their customs, and their institutions. They created a national literature (in both Yiddish and Hebrew) and a flourishing culture: theater, music, art, and eventually film. They also established many institutions of education and scholarship. In addition, through their social concerns and political parties, they contributed greatly to the political and intellectual life of Russian and Polish society.

During World War I, Jews fell victim to the fighting that swept back and forth across Poland. Moreover, in the postwar Poland created by the Treaty of Versailles, anti-Semitism persisted. Pogroms broke out. A right-wing extremist assassinated the first president of the Polish Republic, who, although he was not a Jew, had been elected with the help of Jewish votes in Parliament. Between the wars, the Polish government upheld the principle of equal rights for Jews in theory more than in practice. Inspired by their German neighbors, extremists harassed and persecuted Jews. In the universities, quotas were used against them, and in the classrooms Jews were forced to sit on separate "ghetto benches."

The Polish attitude toward Jews was reflected openly in the government's refusal in 1938 to renew the passports of Polish Jews residing in Germany. When the Nazis initiated their campaign of violence and terror against the Polish Jews, they were doing so in a country with a very long history of anti-Semitism.

The Nazi Persecution of the Jews of Poland

WHEN THE GERMANS INVADED POLAND, they unleashed on its large Jewish population all the pent-up fury and brutality that seven years of Nazi indoctrination had created. Nazi officials poured into Poland behind the invading armies to carry out Hitler's policy. The slogan painted on the side of some of the trains was "We're going to Poland to beat up the Jews."

It was the S.S., under Himmler and Heydrich, who were responsible for the fate of the Jews and the Poles. As soon as Poland had been defeated, Heydrich met with the other top S.S. leaders to plan the country's future. They set up special groups, called *Einsatzgruppen,* to carry out Nazi racial plans. Hitler had already indicated that he wanted the areas of Poland that would be added to Germany "cleansed of Jews, Polacks, and company." Polish children who were judged "racially valuable" because they were blond and looked like Germans were sent to Germany, where they were "Germanized." The rest—Jews and Poles who did not look German—were dumped into the General Government (Nazi-administered central Poland), where the Jews were required to wear armbands.

The Einsatzgruppen were given orders to murder the Polish leadership—labor leaders, government officials, intellectuals, teachers, journalists, clergymen, nobility—and to prepare the rest of the population for slave labor. The numerous Jews of the General Government were to be removed from the countryside and from the thousands of little villages they had lived in for centuries. They were forced into concentrated areas (soon to be ghettos) in the larger cities, preferably near railroad lines "so as to facilitate subsequent measures."

Wherever the Germans went in the cities and villages of Poland, they immediately subjected the Jews to brutal assault. They burned, vandalized, plundered, and desecrated. They dragged Jews from their homes to abuse, beat, and murder them, often with Poles rounded up to watch. In the cities, the Germans looted, ransacked, and closed down Jewish retail stores and confiscated Jewish businesses. They robbed Jews of their valuables, and sometimes they took hostages to force other Jews to turn in their gold or jewelry, and then murdered the hostages instead of releasing them.

The S.S. set the pace and tone of the terror unleashed on the Polish Jews. One winter night, they forced thousands out of their homes into a public square where they beat them and left them to stand overnight. They tortured young girls after sexually abusing them. S.S. officers amused themselves by forcing old Jews to pull them around in carts.

The Jews who wore the traditional long coat and hat—rabbis, rabbinical students, and the orthodox—were subject to especially sadistic attacks. Their attackers kicked them, beat them, and spit on them. They cut off, pulled out, and set their beards and earlocks on fire. Sometimes when the Germans hacked off the beards with their bayonets, they would take off parts of the chin and face as well. The Germans also liked to force religious Jews to set fire to their synagogues or their Torah scrolls.

The Jews who survived this abuse had to face the new terror of forced labor. They were randomly seized to clean streets, scrub floors, haul trash, or do any other menial jobs. In the General Government, the Nazi administrator Hans Frank issued an order that made forced labor compulsory for all Jews between the ages of fourteen and sixty. Labor camps were built outside the cities, and soon the S.S. had 125 labor camps for Jews, where beating, torture, and murder were commonplace. Two of these camps—Treblinka and Majdanek—later became extermination camps.

The Ghettos

THE NAZIS GENERALLY ESTABLISHED THE ghettos in the areas of the old "Jewish quarters." Jews living outside were driven from their homes and forced to live in the cramped quarters of these ghettos, located in the larger cities.

The first ghetto was created in Lodz, Poland's second largest city, in April 1940. The Warsaw ghetto, which came to have a teeming population of five hundred thousand Jews, was created in October. Ghettos in Lublin and other Polish cities were completed in 1941. When Germany launched its attack on the Soviet Union in June 1941, even more ghettos for Jews were created in the conquered cities of Vilna, Bialystok, and Riga.

The Germans used the Jews themselves to administer and facilitate Nazi policies. In each city they set up a "Council of Jewish Elders," called a *Judenrat*. These councils were forced to oversee the evacuation of Jews from the countryside, to provide food to them en route, to find them housing in the cities, and to keep records of the Jews under their supervision. As in Germany, Jewish property and business enterprises were "Aryanized" as quickly as possible.

All the Jewish ghettos were eventually "closed." Their inhabitants were shut off from the rest of the city, and the death penalty was decreed for any Jew found beyond the ghetto walls—on the

"Aryan" side. The overcrowding became frightful. Epidemics and starvation were rampant, especially after the Germans decided that famine was an efficient means of reducing the Jewish population in these ghettos.

The ghetto was increasingly cut off from the outside world. The Germans seized radios, removed telephones, and confiscated packages of food and clothing sent from abroad. In the congestion of these ghettos, people had no privacy or quiet. One girl in the Warsaw ghetto described the atmosphere: "My ears are filled with deafening clamor of crowded streets and cries of people dying on the sidewalks. Even the quiet hours of the night are filled with the snoring and coughing of those who share the same apartment or, only too often, with shots and screams coming from the streets!"

As the Germans cut the food ration to an absolute minimum, bread, potatoes, and fat became the diet of the ghetto—with the occasional possibility of smuggled horsemeat or rotting fish. Starvation and sickness took an increasing number of lives. Jewish refugees from the provinces, many of whom were forced to live in the streets, were usually the first to succumb. People starving or dead in the streets became a common sight. Every day a cart had to go through the streets to pick up the bodies. Describing the Lublin ghetto, a journalist wrote:

> *The congestion, the stench, the poverty, the disease and the chaos which reign in Lublin cannot be paralleled anywhere on earth. Men live in the streets, in cattle stalls, in cellars, in carts and in the debris of devastated houses.*
>
> *Men die like flies in the thoroughfares, their bodies strewn on the roadway like old cinders. . . . The water has turned foul and cannot be drunk. All the wells have been polluted. Cholera and typhus were already rampant when we reached Lublin. . . . The communal soup kitchen can actually serve nothing but potato broth and stale, black bread. Hundreds have not slept for weeks, cramped and confined in noisy freight cars. They wander about sad-eyed and distraught, like mourners at funerals.*

The Nazis ruled these ghettos from the outside by means of the Jewish councils whom they appointed. The Jewish Council of Warsaw consisted of twenty-four members, all picked by the Germans. These Jews were in charge of food rationing, public kitchens, taxes, and the Jewish police force of one thousand men. They were also in charge of supplying the Germans with work gangs. Some gangs marched off early every morning for a full day at a work project outside the ghetto. Others were employed in shops and factories that enterprising Germans set up in the larger ghettos. Such employment for a Jewish worker in the ghetto meant better food, exemption from forced labor, and later it would provide at least temporary protection from deportation to the death camps.

Yet through all the hardship and degradation, the will to live remained strong. The traditional optimism of the Jewish people prevailed. The hope that somehow the nightmare would end never died; the suicide rate was surprisingly low in the ghettos. People strove to keep up their art, literature, music, education, and religion. The Jews maintained underground papers and theaters, and even scientific research, right up to the end. Many took as their own the motto that one group had inscribed on the wall of their synagogue: "For the sake of Heaven, Jews, don't despair."

Jews in the West

NO SOONER HAD HITLER CONQUERED Poland than he ordered his generals to prepare for the invasion of western Europe. On September 3, 1939, England and France declared war on Germany, as they had promised they would if Poland were attacked. However, that winter there was no action on the western front, and newspapers began calling it the "phony war." However, in the spring of 1940, Germany struck with full force to the north and west—into Denmark and Norway in April and into Holland, Belgium, and France in May. On June 21, 1940—after just six weeks of fighting—France surrendered.

The Jews who came under Nazi control in the west were far fewer in number than the Jews of Poland. Furthermore, they had the political rights of other citizens and, like the Jews of Germany, they lived in the midst of their neighbors; they were not set off in any way by their language, dress, or appearance. The anti-Jewish measures taken by the Nazis were more difficult to enforce here, although the western Jews' ultimate fate was to be the same as that of the Jews in the east.

France was divided into the occupied northern part (including Paris), which was under direct German military rule, and the southern "Free Zone," ruled by a French government at Vichy that followed Nazi orders. In both the occupied and "free" parts of France, the Nazis used the French police to carry out their plans for the Jews.

At first, Vichy needed no prodding from the Nazis. On October 3, 1940, the government barred Jews from public life and the press. They were excluded from social and economic life as well, and their property and businesses were "Aryanized." Vichy was much harder on foreign Jews than on those who had lived in France for generations. In the summer of 1940, the Vichy government imprisoned thirty thousand foreign Jews in camps where the able-bodied were drafted for "work battalions."

In occupied France, an S.S. Eichmann aide and his staff set up their office in Paris, where they directed their program of isolating the French Jews from the rest of the population. They registered Jews and established an "Anti-Jewish Institute" for propaganda against them. In 1941 Polish Jews in France were interned, and the transit camp at Drancy was set up for later deportations to the east. In 1942 Jews were put under a curfew, they were forced to wear the yellow Star of David, and they were barred from theaters, movie houses, stores, and other public places.

French Jews were as doomed as their counterparts in the east, but the possibilities of escaping were greater. French Jews who had lived in France for a long time blended more easily into the population, and many were hidden or able to flee. Nuns and monks sheltered numerous Jewish children for the course of the war. And where the Germans did not rule directly, as was the case in the Free Zone of Vichy, the authorities were neither as efficient nor as zealously committed to the job of rounding up Jews to transport them east.

The Jews of Holland (150,000) and Belgium (90,000) were also subjected to harsh anti-Jewish measures. In Holland, Nazis forbade the Jews to set foot in non-Jewish houses, to ride bicycles, or to buy fish or fruit. Dutch Jews were concentrated in certain areas of

Amsterdam, making their eventual round-up and deportation all the more certain. The family of Anne Frank (whose diary was recovered after the war and published) spent two years hiding in Amsterdam, but in 1944 the Nazis discovered their hiding place and sent them off to concentration camps (Anne died in Bergen-Belsen).

After the war began, Nazis subjected the Jews remaining in Germany to more anti-Jewish legislation and propaganda. They had to wear the yellow star, and Germans were forbidden to appear in public with Jews—not that many wanted to do so at this point. Jews were forbidden to use public transportation, and they were not allowed to stop or even slow down when they were out on the street. They were even prohibited from owning pets. At any time, the Nazis might send them off to work camps. Nazis allowed them a food ration of only the barest minimum. To the end of the war, propaganda continued at an hysterical level against the "Jewish menace."

In the fall of 1941, the deportation of Germany's remaining Jews began. The only question in the Nazi crusade to make Germany "pure" and "free of Jews" centered around the status of the *Mischlinge* (those who were part Jewish). Some argued that half Jews should be kept in Germany because their German blood made them natural leaders with superior intelligence, and therefore they would be dangerous if introduced into the "enemy camp."

Finally, after much debate, the Nazis decided that they would include half Jews (Mischlinge, first degree) in the deportations. The only way they could escape this fate was to submit to "voluntary" sterilization. Jews married to Germans were also to be deported, but only after a divorce had been exacted. As for the "one-fourth Jews" (Mischlinge, second degree), they were allowed to keep their status as Germans so long as they did not look or act like Jews.

–10–
The
"Final Solution"

On June 22, 1941—less than two years after Germany promised not to go to war with the Soviet Union by signing the Nazi-Soviet Pact—the German armies struck with devastating force against the Soviet Union. Before the winter set in, they had advanced deep into Russia, to the very gates of Moscow and Leningrad, and deep into the Ukraine as well. It was the final chapter of Hitler's "holy war" against "Jewish Bolshevism" and the vast Slavic nation that Hitler believed the Jews controlled.

In December 1941 Japan, Germany's ally, attacked the United States at Pearl Harbor, and Germany declared war on the United States as well. What had begun as a European war had now engulfed the entire world; it was the bloodiest and most destructive war the world had ever seen.

The Killing Squads

The Nazis' true intentions for the Jews only became clear as they made preparations to invade Russia. While the Jews in Poland were being herded into ghettos, where many died of starvation, disease, and exhaustion, the Nazis were planning a more direct means to murder the Jews of the Soviet Union.

Himmler and Heydrich prepared for the attack on Russia by training special "killing squads"—four of them, numbering about a thousand men each. Their special task was to follow the army into Russia and to kill all Jewish people they found behind the lines.

These squads were modelled on those first used by the Nazis in Poland.

The intensive and highly secret training, involving target practice and Nazi indoctrination, began in Germany in May 1941. The several thousand men who joined these Einsatzgruppen (killing squads) came from the ranks of the S.S. and various other branches of the security police. The importance of their mission to kill Communist leaders, political commissars, and all Jews was stressed. Heydrich told them that "Judaism in the East is the source of Bolshevism and must therefore be wiped out in accordance with the Führer's aims." He also stressed how important it was that the Jewish children be killed as well, so that they would not grow up to become avengers and carriers of the Jewish Bolshevik disease. As one of the officers explained in court after the war, "otherwise children whose parents had been killed, when they grew up, would constitute no less a danger than their fathers."

The Einsatzgruppen officers were generally well educated, and they were all completely dedicated to Nazi ideas about race, Marxism, and Jews. Among the twenty-two who were put on trial after the war, there were eight lawyers, a professor, a dental surgeon, an architect, an art expert, and a former clergyman.

The commanders of the four groups (designated A, B, C, and D) all held the rank of S.S. General. Each group was subdivided into "commandos," and these in turn were broken down into "special commandos." When the German armies drove into Russia in June 1941, the four Einsatzgruppen followed closely behind. Einsatzgruppe A operated in the Baltic countries; B followed the army toward Moscow; C went into the Ukraine; D drove even farther south into the Crimea and other areas of the southern Ukraine. The German armies penetrated deep into Russia so quickly that these "special action groups" had to do most of their slaughtering on their way back from the front, moving from east to west.

These killing squads would first try to get the native populations to do their killing for them. As one Einsatzgruppe put it, "It was necessary to show the world that the native population itself took the initiative in reacting against Jews." The Germans won the services of various Ukrainians, Lithuanians, and Latvians, whom they employed as auxiliaries and later used for such jobs as guards in the death camps.

However, the vast bulk of the killing was done by the Einsatz-gruppen themselves. Based on the methods of deceit, terror, and organized murder worked out back in Germany, their approach was effective against a population suddenly engulfed by German armies and unaware of the Nazis' full intentions.

Most of the squads worked in the same fashion. When they went into a village or town, they would seek out the leading Jews, including rabbis, and tell them to form a council. A day or two later, the Einsatzgruppe would tell the Jewish leaders that they were to gather all the Jews together for "resettlement" to a "Jewish territory" elsewhere. Jews were told that their luggage was not to exceed forty pounds and that food would be provided for them en route. They were then put on trucks or trains or, more often than not, they were led outside town to a location near a ravine or a deep anti-tank ditch. There the Nazis stripped them of their money, valuables, and often even their clothing. They were forced to stand or kneel in a row, whereupon the Nazis shot them and threw their corpses into the ditch. This was the usual procedure, but some squads made their victims climb down on top of the bodies already there and then shot them. There were some instances of Jews burned alive by the squads, and along the Black Sea there were mass drownings.

By 1942 "gas trucks" began appearing in Russia. These trucks could hold about fifty people, and the carbon monoxide of the exhaust fumes was piped into the interior of the truck to suffocate the people inside. But the Nazis never used these trucks extensively. The killing squads preferred the method of lining their victims up along the edge of a ditch and shooting them. One of the commanders said after the war that shooting was the most "humane" method.

The killing campaign in the east was highly secret, and very few Jews escaped. Of those who did escape, even fewer lasted through the war. Therefore, few eyewitness accounts of these mass shootings survived. One of them came from a young mother by the name of Rivka Yosselevscha from the village of Zagrodski. Here is part of what she told a court after the war:

> *When it came to our turn, our father was beaten. We prayed, we begged with my father to undress, but he would not undress; he*

*wanted to keep his underclothes. He did not want to stand naked.
Then they tore the clothing off the old man and he was shot. I
saw it with my own eyes. And then they took my mother and shot
her too; and then there was my grandmother, my father's mother,
standing there; she was eighty years old and she had two children in
her arms. And then there was my father's sister. She also had
children in her arms and she was shot on the spot with the babies in
her arms. . . . We were already facing the grave. The Germans
asked, "Who do you want me to shoot first?" I did not answer. I felt
him take the child from my arms. The child cried out and was shot
immediately. And then he aimed . . . and shot at me. Then I fell to
the ground into the pit amongst the bodies, but I felt nothing . . . I
thought I was dead, that this was the feeling which comes after
death. Then I felt I was choking; people falling over me. I tried to
move and felt that I was alive and that I could rise. I was
strangling. I heard the shots and I was praying for another bullet
to put an end to my suffering, but I continued to move about. I felt
that I was choking, strangling, but I tried to save myself, to find
some air to breathe, and then I felt that I was climbing towards the
top of the grave above the bodies. I rose, and I felt the bodies pulling
at me with their hands, biting at my legs, pulling me down, down.
And yet with my last strength I came up on top of the grave, and
when I did, I did not know the place, so many bodies were lying all
over, dead people . . . They were lying, all dying; suffering; not all
of them dead, but in their last sufferings; naked; shot, but not
dead.*

Such survivors were rare. These Nazi killing squads succeeded in
methodically destroying all the old Jewish communities of Russia.
Of the six million Jews whom the Germans murdered during World
War II, an estimated one and a half million of them were killed by
these Einsatzgruppen.

Preparations for the "Final Solution"

ON JANUARY 20, 1942, HIGH-LEVEL NAZIS in charge of the various
agencies and departments of the government met at a villa in Am
Grossen Wannsee, in suburban Berlin, to plan and implement the
"final solution." Göring had put Heydrich in charge, but it was left

to Adolf Eichmann and his staff, with the help of the foreign office in the various countries of German-occupied Europe, to round up and transport Jews to the death camps in Poland. Up to this time, the killing of Jews had been done piecemeal by special S.S. units, but from this day on, the mass murder of the Jews of Europe became the official (but still secret) policy of the German government.

When the Nazis began to make their plans for the destruction of the rest of the European Jews—the "final solution" to the Jewish problem, as they referred to it in their reports—they already had the example and expertise of Hitler's "Euthanasia Program," which he started in 1939.

Based on Hitler's dream of a "racially healthy" Germany, the project began by identifying and then killing off (usually by injection) German children judged by Nazi "experts" to be mentally ill or physically deformed (about five thousand children were put to death in this way). Later in the year, the project was expanded to include mentally ill adults, who were sent in S.S. vans to one of the six "euthanasia centers" set up in Germany. In groups of twenty to thirty, the victims were led into a hermetically sealed chamber, believing that they were going to take a shower, and were gassed with carbon monoxide. Small crematories had been built to dispose of the bodies. When the Nazis went on to build their death camps in Poland, they used these same techniques.

The project was also extended to the concentration camps inside Germany. There the victims were people considered mentally or physically unfit, usually Jews or other non-Aryans who were too sick to work. At first, the victims were transported to the euthanasia centers, but when they became too crowded, each concentration camp was equipped with its own gas chamber.

Despite all the secrecy surrounding the program, the public eventually found out. Because of the rising disapproval, Hitler suspended his pet project in August 1941 (it is estimated that the project caused between eighty thousand and one hundred thousand deaths). But he did not abandon it entirely. Its personnel, expertise, and some of its equipment were sent to Poland to aid in Hitler's more urgent mission to exterminate the large numbers of Jews languishing in Polish ghettos.

The S.S. chief in Lublin, Odilo Globocnik, was put in charge of eliminating the Jews in central Poland. The head of one of the German euthanasia centers became his chief assistant. In all, ninety-two men from Hitler's euthanasia program moved to Poland to supervise the building of extermination centers. Even some of the very gas chambers used in the program were packed up and sent to Poland.

During the summer of 1941—at the same time the Einsatzgruppen were penetrating deep into Russia on the heels of the advancing German armies—the Nazis built their first extermination camps in Poland. Chelmno, located in the part of Poland annexed by Germany, was the first to be finished and made operational, on December 8, 1941. It had no permanent gas chambers but, rather, a big garage with several "gas trucks." By using the engine exhaust gases of these vehicles, Chelmno could gas up to a thousand people a day.

Belzec, an extermination camp built near Lublin, began its work of killing several thousand people a day in early 1942. Sobibor, also near Lublin, was built in the spring of 1942. Treblinka, a labor camp, fifty miles northeast of Warsaw, was transformed into an extermination camp in July 1942, intended for the killing of Jews in the Warsaw ghetto. The work camp at Majdenek near Lublin was also turned into an extermination camp, giving it the dual purpose of slave labor and annihilation.

Globocnik and the team of "euthanasia experts" that had been sent to him from Germany were in charge of all these extermination camps. They experimented with different methods of gassing, using either gas trucks (also available to the killing squads in Russia) or permanent installations utilizing exhaust gases or prussic acid.

The gassing during these early days was crude and inefficient. One chemist with the S.S. left behind him an informative account of his experience at Belzec during this early experimental phase of the extermination program. In it he recounted a highly secret trip he made, transporting a large amount of prussic acid from Berlin to Lublin, and then on to the Belzec camp with Globocnik the following day. There he witnessed a gassing of a group of Jews from Lemberg, which took over three hours because of a malfunctioning of the camp's diesel engine.

The concentration camp near the little town of Auschwitz, which the Nazis transformed into an extermination camp, eventually became the largest of the Nazi death camps. In a remote, swampy area, it had been started as a concentration camp for German criminals, but when the Nazis sent more and more Poles there, German industries began building factories near the camp to take advantage of the slave labor.

In May 1940 Rudolf Höss, a Nazi Party member since 1922 and a member of the S.S. "Death's Head" Division since 1934, was made commandant of the camp. After the war, he testified that in June 1941 he was called to Berlin and received orders from Hitler to proceed with the "final solution" to the Jewish problem in Europe. Situated in a sparsely settled area near the junction of four railway lines, Auschwitz seemed an ideal site for an extermination camp. Himmler ordered Höss to proceed immediately, thus putting him in direct "competition" with Globocnik's team of "euthanasia experts" at work at Belzec, Treblinka, and the other Polish death camps.

Höss did in fact develop the best method. He conceived of using a gas with a prussic acid base called Zyklon B, which had originally been used to disinfect the huts and barracks of the camp. The first experimental gassings at Auschwitz were carried out in September 1941 on 250 patients from the camp hospital and 600 prisoners of war.

At about this same time, two farm buildings near the hamlet of Birkenau were made airtight and equipped with solid wooden doors. There, about 70,000 Russian prisoners were gassed, and since no crematories had been built yet, their bodies were burned out in the open.

In the meantime, Auschwitz grew into a huge complex of slave labor camps with a population of 150,000, guarded by more than 3000 S.S. troops. Tens of thousands of Jews and non-Jews worked in factories manufacturing artificial rubber and synthetic gasoline, in the armament works, in the surrounding coal mines, and in various smaller factories, farms, and work camps.

It was not until June 1942, however, that the gassing of Jews began on a large scale. Train convoys from all over Europe, packed with Jewish men, women, and children, converged daily on Auschwitz. To handle the increased traffic, four large gas chambers were built, each with adjacent crematories. The Nazis lengthened the railroad tracks to allow the train convoys—sometimes four a day—to bring their cargo right up to the gas chambers.

By 1943 and 1944, the forty-six ovens of the crematories were able to incinerate about twelve thousand bodies a day. By the spring and summer of 1944—when the Nazis were exterminating Jews from Hungary—the death rate increased to twenty-two thousand in one twenty-four hour period. It has been estimated that two million people—most of them Jews—were gassed at Auschwitz alone, while tens of thousands more were worked to death in its slave labor camps.

Deportations

"RESETTLEMENT FOR WORK IN THE EAST" was now the lie the Nazis used to lure the Jews of Europe to their fate. Undertaken with the utmost secrecy, the deportations relied on deceit and terror at every step along the way. Jewish families were made to believe that this "resettlement" would mean a better life. They were even allowed to take along some of their personal belongings. Many believed that they would be put to work repairing the war damage in Poland and Russia. Starving Jews in the Polish ghettos who presented themselves for "resettlement" were lured there by the offer of food. The Germans even forced some deportees to fill out postcards about their life in the east, which were sent back to the ghettos.

The schedule for the transportation of European Jews to the death camps was determined in March 1942. On March 27, Goebbels wrote in his diary, "Beginning with Lublin, the Jews in the General Government are now being evacuated eastward. The procedure is a pretty barbaric one and not to be described here more definitely. Not much will remain of the Jews."

Hitler's early dream of making Germany *Judenrein* (free of Jews) was given top priority. Even before the extermination camps were built, the remaining Jews of greater Germany—Germany, Austria, Bohemia, and Moravia—were transported to eastern ghettos. Germany kept certain skilled Jewish workers until 1943, when its factories were "swept." The last of Germany's Jews, deported in

1942–1943, were sent directly to Auschwitz, although a few "privileged" transports went there via Theresienstadt.*

In the ghettos, any Jews who resisted the forced evacuations were massacred on the spot. The brutality of these "actions," as the Germans liked to call them, helped expedite the process of assembling the Jews and packing them into waiting trains or trucks. Most of the ghettos, especially the larger ones, required a series of such forced evacuations.

The Warsaw ghetto was by far the largest of the ghettos. The deportations there began on July 22, 1942, and continued into the fall until most of its inhabitants (310,322 was the official German count) had been sent off to the extermination camp at Treblinka. That summer, similar "actions" were taken against the other ghettos until, by the end of 1942, an estimated five-sixths of the Jews of Poland had been deported to the death camps. Only those working in slave labor camps, or in the industries the Germans maintained in some of the ghettos, were spared—but not for long.

In 1943 the Germans began "liquidating" the ghettos in Poland, as well as those that had been set up farther east. The Lodz ghetto lasted the longest. In August 1944, the last of its seventy thousand Jewish workers were sent to Auschwitz.

A number of these final deportations were met by fierce Jewish resistance, the strongest of which was the Warsaw ghetto uprising in the spring of 1943. In the early morning hours of April 19, a force of two thousand S.S. troops, armed with tanks, artillery, and machine guns, entered the ghetto to "liquidate" it. Much to their surprise, they met with heavy resistance and, by the end of the day, they were forced to withdraw with heavy casualties. That night— the first night of Passover—the young Jewish fighters, who for months had been arming themselves with homemade weapons, were jubilant. But they were also realistic. They knew the Germans would be back in force, and they had no illusions about the outcome.

Theresienstadt was a Nazi "model" concentration camp in Czechoslovakia. It was made to look like a harmless Jewish "village," and the Germans actually let certain foreigners visit it. For most of its inmates, however, it was but a stopping place on the way to Auschwitz.

Nonetheless, the fighting raged on; it was the first large civilian uprising against the Nazi rule in Europe. Having hoped for a swift liquidation of the ghetto, the Nazis were furious and followed the reports anxiously. On May 1, Goebbels noted in his diary: "This joke isn't going to last long. But one sees what the Jews can do when they are armed."

Relentlessly, block by block, the German armed forces wore down the resistance until, on May 16, the S.S. commander dynamited the big synagogue, which symbolized Jewish life in the ghetto, and withdrew his troops. In the final report he made to his superior in Cracow that night, he proudly declared: "The Jewish quarter of Warsaw is no more!"*

There was resistance elsewhere as well. In the small ghettos, the resistance had to be spontaneous, desperate, and ultimately suicidal, but in the larger ghettos, there was more time to organize. In Bialystok, Vilna, and Kovno, underground combat organizations resisted bravely. Some who survived were able to escape into the forests to fight on as best they could against the Germans.

In the meantime, Eichmann and his agents were fanning out all over Europe to implement the goals of the "final solution." In the countries that the Germans conquered and ruled over directly, the Jews were completely at their mercy. In Holland, for example, despite many courageous attempts by Dutch people to protect their Jewish neighbors, 110,000 of the country's 140,000 Jews were deported to death camps in the course of the war. In fact, one of the greatest ironies of the Holocaust is that Jews who lived in countries that were either allies or satellites of Nazi Germany had a better chance of survival—at least for awhile.

In Free France (the southern half not ruled directly by the Germans), the Nazis could not round up French Jews on their own. They had to rely on the local police and the officials of the Vichy government. While that government wrote its own severe anti-Jewish laws and was only too happy to rid the area of foreign Jews, it was more reluctant to denounce its own Jewish citizens, who had

---

*During the uprising, he kept careful count of the "Jews, bandits, and subhumans" destroyed each day. Now he was able to conclude his final report: "The total number of Jews apprehended and destroyed, according to the record, is 56,065."

been assimilated into French life for generations. This protection of French Jews ended, however, when the German army moved into southern France in response to the Allied invasions of North Africa.

Italy was Germany's closest ally, but it refused to deport its own Jewish citizens, despite intense pressure from the Germans. In fact, Italian zones in southeastern France, Greece, and Croatia (part of Yugoslavia) provided fleeing Jews with a measure of safety, however temporary. This situation changed with the downfall of Mussolini and the German army's occupation of Italy, during which Eichmann's agents hunted down and deported to Auschwitz about a fifth of Italy's forty thousand Jews.

The fate of Hungary's 800,000 Jews was similar. Their protection, too, was ended by German occupation late in the war. Until 1944 Hungary had steadfastly refused to allow the German "experts" to take charge of its Jews. However, when Hungary became reluctant to do battle with the approaching Russians, the German armies rushed in, with Eichmann not far behind. Jumping at the chance to deal with this one remaining large Jewish community, he flew into Budapest to take charge personally. By early summer, he succeeded in rounding up 450,000 Hungarian Jews living outside the capital city and deporting them to Auschwitz. That summer there was a struggle over the fate of Budapest's Jews. Thanks to the work of neutral countries and international agencies, Eichmann's power in Hungary was weakened. The Red Cross and foreign legations in Budapest, especially the Swedes under the leadership of Raoul Wallenberg,* worked frantically to save Jews by issuing thousands of "protection papers." In the confusion of the last months before the arrival of the Russian armies, more than 100,000 of the Jews of Budapest were saved from extermination.

---

*Raoul Wallenberg worked tirelessly to protect Jews and is credited with saving thousands of lives. After the liberation of Budapest, the Russians arrested Wallenberg, suspecting that he was an American spy. He was never seen again. Although the Russians say that he died in their custody a long time ago, there are those who claim that he is still alive and in prison. In 1981 Congress made him an honorary citizen of the United States as a tribute to his heroic work, thus putting pressure on the Soviets to release him—if he is still alive.

Death Camps

AT FOUR OF THE SIX EXTERMINATION centers the Nazis built in Poland, the Jews were transported there by trains or trucks and sent directly to the gas chambers. However, at Majdanek and Auschwitz, which were slave labor camps as well as extermination centers, there were "selections" to supply people for the work gangs. At Auschwitz these selections were made by S.S. doctors right at the station platform after the trains arrived. With a wave of the hand, they would send to the left those to be assigned to labor details—and to the right those who were to die.

To be assigned to the right column—the fate of the children, the elderly, and all but the healthiest looking adults—was to be consigned to immediate extermination. While the old and sickly were taken by trucks, the rest were marched off to a place where the S.S. told them they were going to be disinfected. They went into "dressing rooms," where they undressed and put their clothes on hooks with numbers they were told to remember. After being given bars of soap for their "shower," they were herded into the gas chambers with their simulated showerheads in the ceiling. After the doors were slammed shut and bolted, an S.S. trooper wearing a gas mask would drop Zyklon B gas containers through specially constructed openings in the ceiling.

A half hour later, a special group of Jewish workers—called the *Sonderkommando*—opened the doors at the other end of the chamber. It was their job to dispose of the bodies and make room for the next group. After removing all the gold teeth, rings, and earrings, and cutting off the hair of the women, the workers took the bodies to be burned in the crematories or in the open air. At first, the ashes were dumped into ditches, but later they were taken by truck to a river. One survivor of Auschwitz said that "the stench given off . . . contaminated the surrounding countryside. At night the red sky over Auschwitz could be seen for miles."

The selections of able-bodied workers were especially important at Auschwitz, which expanded into a huge slave-labor complex where tens of thousands of prisoners were put to work in surrounding I.G. Farben factories, Krupp armament works, and scores of other factories, mines, and farms connected to Auschwitz.

Such a "selection," however, meant only a short delay of inevitable death, since hard labor, brutal treatment, and minimum rations awaited those who were selected. The average length of survival at Auschwitz was three months. To last for six months was considered exceptional. Those who survived the initial selection were tattooed on their arms before they joined the ranks of the slave laborers.

That was just the beginning, however, because "partial selections" were constantly taking place among the Jewish prisoners at Auschwitz. Squads of S.S. troopers, headed by the camp doctor, would sweep through the barracks and the camp infirmary at regular intervals to collect new victims for the gas chambers. Their places were immediately filled by new selections from the train convoys arriving every day.

The Nazi concentration camps inside Germany—Buchenwald, Dachau, Bergen-Belsen, Sachsenhausen, Ravensbrück (for women), and others—were originally designated for Communists, socialists, labor leaders, dissident writers and journalists, homosexuals, and common criminals. Although they were not extermination centers as such, life in them was cheap. Some had their own gas chambers and crematories, but death came more often by means of shootings, beatings, injections, starvation, and disease. Buchenwald, for example, had special large rooms for shootings and a camp routine so brutal that hundreds of prisoners died every day.

No matter how terrible the deportations to the camps—in packed trains for days without food and water or room to rest—the shock of arriving at the death camps was overwhelming, often fatally so. Many did not survive that first trauma of seeing their wives, children, and families sent off to the gas chambers, the loss of all their personal belongings, the shaving of their heads, the beatings and shootings of their fellow prisoners, or the filth and vomit.

The camps were deliberately made as horrid as possible, with a regime designed to break the spirit of the prisoners while exploiting their physical labor. The nights in the barracks offered no relief from the nightmare. One survivor described the experience:

> . . . *buckets of excrement stood in a little passage by the exit. There were not enough. By dawn, the whole floor was awash with urine and feces. We carried the filth about the hut on our feet, the stench made people faint.*

Most prisoners could not stand it. Some hastened their end by throwing themselves against electrified fences. Others simply died spiritually and emotionally, becoming the "walking dead." They fell ill, or starved, or stumbled into situations that got them killed. Or they hung on until the next camp selection sent them to the gas chambers.

There were also medical experiments carried out at Auschwitz and in the German concentration camps. Himmler provided camp inmates for research by German scientific institutes, chemical industries, the armed services, and his own S.S. doctors.

At Auschwitz, sterilization experiments were performed on Jewish men and women. The air force used prisoners from the concentration camps to study the effects of freezing water and high altitudes on humans. Some experiments infected prisoners with typhus and other diseases to study new drugs. The prisoners who survived these experiments were usually killed afterwards.

S.S. doctors cut out muscles and bones, removed organs, and introduced cancer into inmate bodies. Those who did not die immediately usually did so shortly afterwards from neglect and excruciating pain. Those few who survived remained maimed and crippled for life.

Desperate uprisings occurred at several of the extermination centers. At Treblinka on August 3, 1943, a carefully planned revolt finally broke out. The prisoners seized weapons from the armory, cut the telephone lines, and set fire to the barracks, watchtowers, the gas chambers, and even the railway station with its false front to calm Jewish misgivings about their "resettlement."

German reinforcements were called in to crush the revolt, and just about all of the seven hundred Jews who were involved were hunted down and killed. One of the survivors described the satisfaction in seeing the camp destroyed: "We realized our aim fully and in martyrdom. Treblinka was wiped out. A fortress of horrible Nazism was erased from the face of the earth."

Two months later, a similar revolt at Sobibor killed about fifty S.S. and Ukrainian guards and forced Himmler to destroy the camp completely.

There was even an uprising at Auschwitz. The Jewish underground in the camp arranged several escapes in a desperate attempt to get word to the Allies about the camp, in hopes of getting them to bomb the camp and its facilities. By 1944 they gave up hope of help from the outside and made a plan to blow up the gas chambers and crematories themselves. By then, the camp was operating at peak capacity to handle the round-the-clock arrival of trainloads of Hungarian Jews. When the Sonderkommando found out that they were all about to be exterminated, they blew up Crematorium III on their own, killing some S.S. soldiers in the process. Several hundred prisoners escaped from the camp in the confusion that followed, but the S.S. set out after them and killed them all.

Late in 1944, the killing at Auschwitz stopped. The S.S. blew up the gas chambers and crematories, burned the camp records, and drove the prisoners back into Germany where they were dumped, diseased and without food, while Hitler made his last stand.

The day before his death in Berlin, Hitler showed, for the last time, the bitter hatred that had consumed him for so long. In the political testament he dictated in his underground bunker—his farewell message to the German people—he blamed the war on "international Jewry." He urged the future leaders of Germany to uphold the racial laws and to ruthlessly oppose Jews as "the universal poisoner of all peoples." Then on the next day—April 30, 1945—this greatest mass murderer in the history of the world escaped the retribution of justice by committing suicide.* With Nazi Germany's surrender a week later, the nightmare of the war in Europe was finally over.

Goebbels, Himmler, and Göring also committed suicide. After the war, Göring was sentenced to death at Nuremberg with some other top Nazis, but he escaped hanging by committing suicide in his cell.

PART IV

CHRONOLOGY · *Part IV*

END OF WORLD WAR II		1946 *Nazi leaders convicted of war crimes at Nuremberg*
		1947 *U.N. votes to partition Palestine*
BIRTH OF ISRAEL		1948 *State of Israel born; War of Independence*
	1950	1949 *Israel admitted to United Nations*
		1952 *26 Soviet Jewish writers executed*
		1953 *Doctors' Plot*
		1953 *Death of Stalin*
		1956 *Arab-Israeli Sinai War*
	1960	1959–1960 *Wave of anti-Semitic incidents in Europe and U.S.*
		1962 *Adolf Eichmann tried and executed*
		1965 *Neo-Nazi National Democratic Party founded in Germany*
		1965 *Second Vatican Council absolves Jews of killing Christ*
ARAB-ISRAELI WARS (Vietnam War era in U.S.)		1967 *Six-Day War*
	1970	1973 *Yom Kippur War*
		1975 *Zionist "racism" condemned by U.N. General Assembly*
		1978 *U.S. Congress passes anti-Arab boycott bill*
	1980	1980 *Explosion at Paris synagogue kills four, injures fifteen*
		1981 *World Gathering of Jewish Holocaust Survivors in Jerusalem*
		1981 *Assassination of Anwar Sadat*

–11–

The Middle East

HITLER MIGHT HAVE LOST THE WAR, but in his fanatical crusade to make Europe "free of Jews," he was largely successful. Most European Jews who did escape or survive the Holocaust have not chosen to go back to live in Europe. Europe is no longer the center of Jewish life it was for so many centuries. Today Jews live all over the world. The three largest Jewish communities are in the United States, the Soviet Union, and Israel. Each one faces unique challenges, and each one faces, in different ways and to varying degrees, old hatreds and new dangers.

Israel sees itself as surrounded by a hostile Arab world that longs to see it destroyed. Israel signed a peace treaty with Egypt in 1978, but still feels friendless and hated by most Arab countries.

Arab Hostility to the Birth of Israel

ARAB OPPOSITION WAS PRIMARILY responsible for the British policy of restricting the number of Jews admitted to Palestine during and immediately after the war, when the need for a refuge was greatest. The policy made it "illegal" for Jews who had escaped the Nazi nightmare, or who had somehow survived the Holocaust, to attempt entering Palestine.

When the British proved unable to manage the pressures from both the Jews and the Arabs, the United Nations Special Committee on Palestine came up with a proposal to divide Palestine into a Jewish state, an Arab state, and a small internationally administered zone, which included Jerusalem. This recommendation was supported by both the United States and the Soviet Union. On November 29, 1947, it was adopted by the necessary two-thirds of the member states of the United Nations General Assembly—with Britain abstaining and the Arabs walking out in protest.

The Arabs were determined to strangle the infant nation in its crib. The very day the state of Israel was proclaimed—May 14, 1948—the armies of five Arab states (Egypt, Jordan, Lebanon, Syria, and Iraq) attacked their young neighbor. The Jews were prepared, however, having procured arms to defend themselves in the intervening months. In the fighting, they gained footholds in new territory. They did lose control of the Old City of Jerusalem, but they held onto the New City. There was a truce, but in four weeks the fighting resumed. On July 18, a new cease-fire was arranged and armistice agreements were made in January 1949. As a result of this opening War of Independence, Israel survived and increased its original territory by about half. Elections were held for the Knesset (Parliament), and a government was formed with David Ben-Gurion as prime minister and Chaim Weizmann as president. On May 11, 1949, Israel was admitted to the United Nations, but was still unwelcome in the Arab world—a world that forced Israel to grow up in an atmosphere of constant seige and military preparedness—as evidenced by wars in 1956, 1967, and 1973.

Even before Israel was born, the Arab states, organized into the Arab League in 1944, instituted an economic boycott against the Jews of Palestine. The boycott put a ban on "Jewish products and manufactured goods" and urged all Arabs "to refuse to deal in or consume Zionist products." After the Arabs failed to crush the new state in 1948, they intensified their economic campaign. They extended their boycott to companies in Europe and the United States that did business with Israel. They widened it further by boycotting companies that did business with those companies already blacklisted for trading with Israel. The Suez Canal was closed to Israeli shipping and to the ships headed for Israeli ports from other countries.

Arab Anti-Semitism

IN EUROPE AFTER WORLD WAR II, anti-Semitism was muted by the sheer horror of the Holocaust and its aftermath. However, no such taboo was present in Arab countries, and as a result of the Arab-Israeli conflict, anti-Semitic propaganda against the Jewish state was rampant. ("Anti-Semitic" is an awkward term to use when speaking about Arabs, because the Arab peoples are also "Semitic".)

Arabs aimed their attacks not just at Israel or "Zionists"; they aimed them at Jews and Judaism. The outspoken hatred emanated not from the fringes of Arab society, but from its very center—from the highest levels of government and the media it controlled.

In the Arab world, *Protocols of the Elders of Zion* became popular once again. A number of translations and editions appeared, and Arab leaders referred to it frequently. President Gamal Nasser of Egypt found it "very important" to understanding the Zionist threat, and to this day Colonel Muammar el Qaddafi of Libya keeps a copy of this "most important document" at his desk. Excerpts from it have been used in Arab school textbooks and in indoctrination manuals for the armed forces.

During World War II, the Grand Mufti of Jerusalem, Haj Amin al-Husseini, had supported the Nazis, and afterwards Hitler's approach to the Jews was still regarded favorably. One Jordanian writer, Abdallah al-Tall, contended that Hitler had been "wronged and slandered" for trying to deal with the evil character of Jews. His claim was that Arabs should not have to suffer for what Jews had brought on themselves:

> *The blame (for the massacre of the Jews) applies first and foremost to the Jews themselves and their characteristics of treachery, deceitfulness, crime and treason, and in the second place to European civilization, which apparently could not long suffer the vile Jewish character, and in the course of time hatred of the Jews and loathing for their vices led to a movement of collective killing.*

Another Arab writer recommended close attention to Hitler's ideas: "The truth is that the study of what Hitler wrote on world Zionism has become a vital matter for anyone who lives in the Arab countries after the year 1948." Some Arab leaders went so far as to question publicly whether the Holocaust ever took place, a tactic that has since been used by anti-Semites in different parts of the world. Nasser called the report that six million Jews had been murdered "a lie," and Jordan's prime minister called it "a fable legend." In 1961, at the time of the trial and execution of Adolf Eichmann in Israel (for his key role in rounding up and transporting the Jews of Europe to their destruction), there were voices in the Arab world that hailed him as a martyr.

Even the old "ritual-murder" accusation resurfaced. In 1972 King Faisal of Saudi Arabia told a Cairo newspaper: "Two years ago when I was in Paris, police discovered the bodies of five children. . . . Afterwards it turned out that Jews killed the children to mix their blood into their bread."

This campaign of Arab hatred against Jews caused a number of Arab governments to take it out on their own Jewish population. No sooner did Israel become a state than all the Jews of Iraq were classified as "enemy aliens." The government seized their property and businesses, and prohibited emigration. In 1950, when the ban was lifted for a year, all but 6000 of Iraq's 120,000 Jews fled the country for Israel. Further repressive measures drove more Jews away until just before the Six-Day War in 1967,* when severe restrictions were placed on the citizenship, property, and travel of the 2500 Jews remaining in Iraq. More extreme measures followed the war. The Iraqi government put all Jewish homes under surveillance; telephones were disconnected; assets were frozen; Jews were fired from their jobs; and travel outside the area of their residence was forbidden. In Baghdad, several Jews were hanged, along with Muslim opponents of the regime, as "imperialist and Zionist spies."

Syrian Jews were also restricted. They were forbidden to sell off their property or to move beyond a one-and-a-half-mile radius from their homes without a special permit. They were also required to carry special identity cards. After the Six-Day War, the 4000 Jews of Syria were not allowed to leave the country.

Just before the Six-Day War, Egypt registered its 2500 Jews; within days after the outbreak of hostilities, the government ar-

---

The Six-Day War primarily involved Israel, Egypt, Syria, and Jordan. During the war, Israel occupied land (such as the Sinai Peninsula and the Golan Heights) that has been the cause of disputes and conflicts ever since.

rested most of the community's Jewish men. Most of them were released the following year, but others remained in prison until 1969 or 1970. The Jews of Libya were also restricted and persecuted after the outbreak of the war. When the ban on emigration was lifted, the entire Jewish community left the country. Throughout the Arab world, Jews were made to feel unwelcome.

The Arabs carried their anti-Zionist crusade to the United Nations and other international forums, where they publicly attacked Jews and Israel with a blatant anti-Semitism not heard since the 1930s in Germany. This Arab propaganda war against Israel gained strength and international respectability when it was joined by the Soviet bloc and by a large number of Third World nations.

In November 1975, the campaign against Israel reached a new height when the U.N. General Assembly passed a resolution that condemned Zionism as "a form of racism and racial discrimination." The American ambassador Daniel Patrick Moynihan called the action "infamous" and told the delegates that they were openly endorsing anti-Semitism.

While disagreements with Israel about international policy are hardly proof of anti-Semitism, for many people today anti-Zionism has become but a new and more respectable way of attacking Jews and fanning the flames of anti-Semitism. The miracle of Israel's birth has had its tragically ironic dark side. The creation of a Jewish state was meant to cure anti-Semitism by putting an end to Jewish homelessness and vulnerability. Instead, the seemingly indestructible presence of modern Israel has unleashed anti-Semitic attacks, fresh and forceful, from different corners of the earth.

–12–
The Soviet Union

IN THE TWENTIETH CENTURY, THE plight of the Jews in the Soviet Union has been even worse than it was under the czars. Since 1917 Russian Jews have been stripped of just about everything important to their identity: their religion, their language, and their institutions. Today they are discriminated against more than any other minority in the Soviet Union. Recent intensification of Soviet anti-Zionist propaganda has made Russian Jews feel even more isolated.

Jewish Hopes Crushed

WHEN THE GOVERNMENT OF CZAR NICHOLAS II was overthrown in March 1917, Russian Jews rejoiced. Their hopes for a better life remained high until November, when the Bolshevik Revolution established the Communist dictatorship. The very first decree of the new Provisional Government (set up after the czar's fall) prohibited all discrimination based on ethnic, religious, and social considerations. Shortly afterwards the Ministry of Defense put an end to discrimination against Jews in the army, where they had previously been allowed only as soldiers, not as officers.

Jews renewed their social and political activities—which had been silenced after the start of World War I—with great vigor. A whole range of Jewish political parties and labor organizations joined in the building of a new government, hoping that in the new

Russia Jews would be able to maintain their distinctive life and culture. A conference of Jews from all over Russia opened in Petrograd in August 1917 to discuss the shape that Jewish life would take. Yiddish and Hebrew publications, suppressed by military censors in 1915, reemerged and enthusiastically hailed the new freedom.

However, this "springtime" of hope was short-lived, surviving barely seven months. In November 1917, the Bolsheviks seized power, thus bringing to an end the socialist and liberal regime that had held such great promise for Jews and other Russians. Lenin's dictatorship dashed the Jewish hopes that had been raised in the brief interlude between the fall of czarism and the victory of Bolshevism. One Jewish newspaper summed up the attitude of most Russian Jews: "The Bolshevik coup is madness. It is madness to think that a negligible section of democracy can impose its will on the whole country."

While Lenin and the Bolshevik leaders were not anti-Semitic as such, they believed that for Bolshevism to succeed, no group could separate itself from the rest of the Russian people. Therefore, they were opposed to all expressions of Jewish nationalism, and called for the total integration of Jews into society. Even those leaders who were Jewish themselves, such as Leon Trotsky and Grigori Zinoviev, abandoned Judaism in favor of the principles of the revolution.

For this reason, the new Communist regime proceeded to become more destructive of Russian Jewry than the czars had ever been. Lenin's dictatorship embarked on a program that was to extinguish the religious, cultural, and national life of the Jews of Russia, a life that had somehow survived all those years of czarist persecution, pogroms, and forced emigration.

In 1921 the entire membership of the *Bund,* a Jewish labor union, was officially transferred to the Communist Party. For all practical purposes, the once-thriving Russian Jewish Socialism came to an end, as did the dream of Jewish national and cultural freedom inside Russia.

This Soviet policy of integrating national minorities into the Communist state has been in effect ever since and of course applies to non-Jewish groups as well. But Soviet Jews have been more severely victimized for a number of reasons. First of all, from the beginning of Communist rule, Jews have been attacked by the anti-religious propaganda of the Soviet state. To this day, the government-controlled press carries lurid stories about the alleged immorality and dishonesty of a rabbi or some other Jew, often accompanied by a caricature of this individual, picturing him with a hooked nose and other distinctive "Jewish" features. The effect of such propaganda has been a reinforcement of general anti-Semitism and the impression that the government regards Jews as "fair game" for discrimination and mistreatment.

The fierce anti-Zionist campaign of the government has had a similar effect. Soviet spokesmen (like their Arab counterparts) claim that they are not anti-Semitic but, rather, "anti-Zionist." However, like much anti-Zionism elsewhere in the world, Soviet anti-Zionism—in newspaper articles and cartoons—is accompanied by such bitter hatred of Jews that it is indistinguishable from anti-Semitism. Soviet propaganda, which continually warns the Russian people against the "Zionist world conspiracy" is not very different in tone or content from that earlier product of Russian fear and fantasy—*Protocols of the Elders of Zion.*

Another factor that has separated Jews from other nationalities within the Soviet Union—and made them all the more vulnerable—is that Jews have no territorial base. In 1928 the Soviet government made an attempt to give Soviet Jews a "home" of their own. They chose Biro-Bidzhan, a bleak, barely inhabited piece of land in Siberia, hoping that such a "homeland" might satisfy the Soviet Zionists, at the same time helping to safeguard Russia's Far Eastern frontier with Japan. However, the idea never became popular, so that today only about 9 percent of the people who live there—less than 15,000—are Jewish.

The Soviet Assault against the Jewish Way of Life

THERE HAS BEEN NO MORE DRAMATIC and devastating assault on the traditional life of Russian Jews than the systematic Communist attack on Judaism. The Bolshevik campaign began within months of the establishment of the Soviet state. To implement the "dictatorship of the proletariat" among the Jewish masses, the state abolished the Jewish religious schools: the *heders* (small primary schools), the *Talmud Torahs* (secondary schools), and the *yeshivas* (Talmudic academies). There were even public "show trials" directed against religious institutions and the Talmud that were reminiscent of the Talmud trials in Europe during the Middle Ages.

The campaign against synagogues began in 1923. When they fell into disrepair, the authorities would not let them be repaired. Most were forced to close under the pretext that their premises were needed for other social services—or that they were not houses of worship at all, but clubs for "profiteers." As a result of over sixty years of Communist policy, only several dozen synagogues and prayer houses remain out of the thousands that once existed in czarist Russia.

Jewish cemeteries were desecrated by being converted into public parks or sites for the construction of public buildings. "Proletarian calendars" for Jews pointedly avoided mentioning important Jewish holidays. Jewish Communists ridiculed the "stupidities" of Judaism by holding public banquets on Yom Kippur and conducting mock trials of "bourgeois" rabbis. In 1937–1938, a campaign against "fascist espionage" resulted in the arrest and deportation of numerous rabbis, kosher butchers, and circumcisers. Others in smaller communities were forced to resign, "since there was no longer need for their services."

Thousands of rabbis practiced under the czars, but now only a handful remain. Their average age is over seventy, and they cannot be replaced because there are no seminaries left in the Soviet Union for training rabbis. Jews are not even allowed to publish their own religious materials. No Hebrew Bible has been published since 1917. Not a single Jewish religious book has been printed since the early 1920s.

Any public expression of Zionism has likewise been attacked by the Soviet state. Zionism flourished in Russia before the Revolution, but the Communist Party saw it as an obstacle to the establishment of "the dictatorship of the proletariat" among Jews and criticized it as "a citadel of reaction and counterrevolution."

In 1919 the Soviet secret police suppressed all Zionist publications and arrested Zionist leaders. On the night of September 2, 1934, there was a nationwide crackdown, in which three thousand Zionists were arrested in 150 locations in the U.S.S.R. and were sentenced to three to ten years of slave labor. Hebrew, regarded by the Communists to be a reactionary language, was outlawed in speech and in print, and today it remains the only language that the Soviet Union condemns unconditionally. This ban on Hebrew, instituted to help kill Zionism, makes Hebrew prayer and the study of religious subjects virtually impossible. These last vestiges of underground Zionism ended when its leaders were banished to the labor camps in Siberia.

In addition to its war against Judaism and Zionism, the Soviet state has worked to remove all manifestations of Jewish secular culture as well. After the consolidation of Joseph Stalin's dictatorship in the 1930s, the government shut down all Communist periodicals that were specifically Jewish. Likewise, all Yiddish publications devoted primarily to the history of the Jewish labor movements were confiscated and removed from library shelves. Unlike Lenin, who opposed anti-Semitism and who had many close Jewish comrades, Stalin was deeply suspicious and fearful of Jews as a threat to his personal power and as potential "enemies of the state." In 1938 he launched a purge of leading Jewish figures in the Communist party, which resulted in the liquidation of a whole generation of Jewish intellectuals, historians, writers, journalists, and musicians as "enemies of the people."

From 1948 until his death in 1953, Stalin instituted more purges against Jews in the party ranks. All the remaining Jewish cultural organizations and Yiddish publications were shut down. By the end of 1948, more than four hundred Jewish intellectuals—completely assimilated and loyal Communists who had survived the purges of the 1930s—had been arrested and executed. More purges followed. In August 1952, twenty-six Communist Jewish writers were tried, convicted, and executed. The best Jewish writers of both the younger and the older generations were destroyed, and Yiddish literature, which had once flourished in Russia, was all but obliterated.

One of the most dramatic of these anti-Jewish purges occurred just before Stalin died in 1953. Known as the "Doctors' Plot," it involved the "unmasking" of a group of prominent Moscow doctors, mostly Jews, in an alleged conspiracy to assassinate Soviet leaders. On January 13, the Communist Party newspaper *Pravda* and Radio Moscow announced that nine eminent doctors, six of them Jews, had been arrested and had confessed to murdering two Soviet leaders, who had died in 1945 and 1948, respectively. Authorities reported that they had confessed to conspiring to murder a number of leading figures in the Soviet armed forces. In the weeks that followed, the Soviet press lashed out against Zionism, Israel, imperialism, and Wall Street.

The death of Stalin on March 5, 1953, saved the lives of the accused doctors. The plot had been Stalin's opening move in his plan for yet another purge, but without his direction it could not proceed. On April 3, *Pravda* announced that the doctors were not guilty and that they had been released and, furthermore, that those responsible for using "impermissible means of investigation" had been arrested. In his secret speech to the Twentieth Party Congress in 1956, Nikita Khrushchev blamed the Doctors' Plot on Stalin but refrained from making any critical comments about its anti-Semitic aspects.

The Doctors' Plot trial was just one in a series of anti-Semitic "show trials" that took place in eastern Europe in the last years of Stalin's life. Earlier, there had been a major trial in Czechoslovakia. Rudolf Slánský—who had served as secretary-general of the Czechoslovak Communist Party after World War II—and thirteen other top party leaders were tried and convicted, and all but three of them were executed. Slánský was Jewish, as were ten of the others. In an openly anti-Semitic trial, the Jewish background of the defendants was continually stressed, and the old anti-Semitic charge of a worldwide Jewish conspiracy was loudly proclaimed. This alleged Zionist plot was a common theme of the various purges and trials in the Soviet bloc countries during the last years of Stalin's rule.

After Stalin's death, government-backed anti-Semitism not only continued, but also grew stronger. Anti-religious propaganda directed against Jews became even more harsh.

Soviet propaganda usually portrays Judaism as corrupt and immoral because of its alleged encouragement of "profiteering" and "exploitation." During the early 1960s, Soviet authorities launched a campaign against so-called "economic crimes," singling out Jews as the main culprits. For example, in the Ukraine, where Jews make up 2 percent of the population, 90 percent of those put to death for such crimes were Jews. The government publicized the cases to make it clear to all that the accused were Jewish, either by mentioning the family name or by mentioning details that associated a synagogue or a rabbi with the crime. The crude purpose of this anti-Semitic campaign was to steer "good decent Russians" away from such Jewish "swindlers and crooks."

Soviet Jews have even been denied the right to a public remembrance of the atrocities they suffered at the hands of the Nazis. Russia was the prime killing ground of the *Einsatzgruppen*; it is estimated that one and a half million Soviet Jews were murdered by the Nazis. Yet Soviet monuments never identify Jews, even where Jews were the only victims. Soviet authorities removed monuments from the sites of mass executions of Jewish people and replaced them with other memorials, which referred to the victims only as "innocent Soviet citizens" or "Russians, Ukrainians, and others." In western Russia, a monument erected in 1945 in memory of four thousand Jews killed by the Nazis was later removed and replaced by a public bathroom. At Babi Yar, the ravine outside Kiev where approximately fifty thousand Jews were massacred, there is a monument to "Soviet citizens," but no mention of the Jewish victims.

Soviet anti-Zionist propaganda grew more intense after the 1967 Six-Day War in Israel. Various publications began developing the theory that the millions of Jews killed during World War II were in fact the victims of a "Zionist-Nazi conspiracy." This outrageous idea is a part of the Soviet argument that the Israelis are "the Nazis of our time."

Even the most assimilated, loyal Russian Jews are discriminated against in many areas of Soviet society, and consequently some Soviet Jews wish to emigrate. Under pressure from the United States, over two hundred thousand Russian Jews have left in the last decade to go to Israel or to the West. More have applied to leave but have not yet received permission. Almost always, the very act of applying for an exit visa causes more discrimination against the applicant. Applicants are often fired from their jobs.

Jews are accepted in certain white-collar areas—in theater and law, for example—but they are now excluded or limited at most universities, especially at those in the larger cities. In 1935 the percentage of Jewish students at universities was 13 percent, but thirty years later that figure dropped to 3 percent. Jews are now almost completely absent from all policy-making positions and from the higher ranks of the Communist party, the government, the armed services, and the diplomatic corps.

The fate of the Jews of Russia has been tragic. What was once the most lively, the most populous, and the most creative Jewish community in the world has been decimated by the Nazis and has nearly been "Russified" out of existence by the Soviets. Today, the prospects for those assimilated Russian Jews are not very bright, given Soviet hostility toward Israel and its "Zionist" supporters. However, this adversity has made a number of Russian Jews more self-consciously Jewish. Many, including the young, now want to know much more about Judaism, about Israel, and about their own Jewish roots.

–13–
The Western World

EUROPE WAS THE BREEDING GROUND of the anti-Semitism that resulted in the Holocaust, but even that horror did not put an end to anti-Semitism there. It lived on, even in countries where hardly any Jews remained, and it found young advocates at both ends of the political spectrum.

In eastern Europe, where very few Jewish people remain, there exists an attitude that one writer described as "anti-Semitism without Jews." In these Soviet-bloc countries, the government-controlled media often blame economic problems and other domestic troubles on unnamed "Zionists" and "Zionist agents." In 1980 and 1981 in Poland, for example, at the time of the emergence of Solidarity, the independent trade union, some government officials blamed the unrest on "Zionists." Anti-Semitism lives on in western Europe, too.

Germany

IN GERMANY THERE ARE RELATIVELY few Jews left today. Most of them live in Berlin and a few other large cities. West Germany—created out of that part of Germany occupied after the war by France, Britain, and the United States—has attempted to sever its ties with the past. The new West German government outlawed the Nazi Party, and adopted a policy of payments to Israel and to individual Jewish victims of the Nazi era. Nazis have also been brought to trial in various West German courts, although many former Nazis have been allowed to resume their normal lives in West German society.

Anti-Semitism has persisted under the surface of German life. From time to time, it comes out into the open in the form of the desecration of synagogues and cemeteries with swastikas. On Christmas Eve of 1959, German youths painted a swastika on a synagogue in Cologne. Within days, there was an epidemic of anti-Semitic incidents throughout Germany. They were repeated in hundreds of cities in Europe and the United States, where 643 such acts were reported over two months' time.

Small Nazi-like groups have emerged in Germany from time to time, but so far they have not gathered much support. The most serious such threat was the National Democratic Party, founded by Adolf von Thadden in 1965 and led mainly by ex-Nazis. To stay within the bounds of West German law, the party had to be very careful about saying what it stood for, but its appeal to old fears and prejudices was unmistakable. It attacked Israel viciously and demanded "an end to the lie of Germany's exclusive guilt which serves to extort continuously thousands of millions from our people," a reference to the government's policy of compensation payments to Israel and to individual Jewish victims of Nazism. The party shocked the country and the world when, in the state elections of 1966–1967, it did well enough to gain admission to a number of state parliaments. However, in the 1969 general election, when it failed to win enough votes for admission to the national parliament, the party faded from the political scene.

France

IN FRANCE THE PROBLEM OF ANTI-SEMITISM is a complex one that continues to vex the national conscience. Thanks to the French Revolution, France was the first country to grant Jews citizenship with full and equal political and civil rights. Napoleon became the liberator of Jews in other parts of Europe as well. However, for the rest of the century anti-Semitism became a weapon in the hands of the royalists, the clergy, and the military, as these conservative forces opposed successive republican governments. The struggle intensified at the end of the century with the Dreyfus affair and its outpouring of open anti-Semitism.

To this struggle was added the burden of guilt about France's actions during World War II—its early collapse and surrender to the Germans, the establishment of the puppet Vichy government and, finally, the deportation and extermination of one-quarter of the French Jews. The price of France's surrender was high and, to this day, the French feel a sense of national shame. France did cooperate, however reluctantly, with the German program for the "final solution." French officials drew up lists of French Jews, and French police rounded them up and handed them over to the S.S., who in turn transported them to the gas chambers in the east. On its own, the Vichy government instituted laws against Jews that were more severe than the laws of the Nazis.

The memory of this collaboration and of the wartime fate of the country's Jews has weighed heavily on the national conscience. For many years after the war, any expression of anti-Semitism, or even discussion of the subject, was taboo. In 1967, however, France showed the first signs of loosening this taboo. Shortly after the Six-Day War, President Charles de Gaulle spoke of Jews as "an elite people, sure of itself and dominating." Soon after, French foreign policy began leaning away from Israel toward the support of the Arabs and the Palestine Liberation Organization. In taking up the cause of the Palestinians, French radicals became outspokenly anti-Zionist, giving long-suppressed anti-Semitic feelings a new and more acceptable channel of expression.

Since then, small extremist groups have become more active, and anti-Semitic incidents have become more commonplace in France. The more serious of these incidents have included the murder of Pierre Goldman, an activist and a best-selling author, and the attempted assassination of the widow of Henri Curiel, an exiled Egyptian-Jewish leftist leader, who himself was murdered in France some years earlier by rightist terrorists. There have also been numerous bombings—at a Jewish university students' canteen; at a Jewish child-care center, leaving thirty-two injured; and—most dramatically—in the fall of 1980, at a synagogue in the heart of Paris, leaving four dead and fifteen injured. This murderous bombing resulted in a huge public demonstration. Well over a hundred thousand Parisians took to the streets to protest anti-Semitism.

Some observers of French culture claim that, despite these incidents, anti-Semitism is less prevalent in France today than it has been for some years. Not long ago, a poll showed that 12 percent of the French population thought there were too many Jews in France—but the same poll revealed that 49 percent of these people also thought there were too many North Africans, 28 percent thought there were too many blacks, and 16 percent thought there were too many Spaniards.

Spain

SPAIN IS A COUNTRY WHOSE ANTI-SEMITIC past includes the Spanish Inquisition and the mass expulsion of Jews in 1492. Today very few Jews live in Spain, but recent developments show that anti-Semitism is very much alive.

In January 1979, after the writer Leon Uris's television series about World War II was broadcast in Spain, a group of a hundred Spaniards filed suit against the television network on the grounds that the programs were "racist" because they focused on the mass killing of Jews in the Nazi death camps. In April of that same year, several neo-Nazi youth groups celebrated a Catholic mass honoring Hitler's birthday. At about the same time, three Jewish-owned stores in Madrid were burned. In Barcelona, several Jewish store owners received death threats. In a Barcelona synagogue, a bomb was found, and the walls were covered with anti-Semitic insults, such as "Death to the Jews."

That same year, about twenty thousand ultra-rightists, many of them members of the growing number of neo-Nazi groups, held an illegal and openly anti-Semitic demonstration in Madrid. In the 1979 municipal elections, a fanatical, anti-Semitic right-wing group collected one hundred thousand votes in Madrid alone. After an edited version of the television series *Holocaust* was shown on Spanish television, a Nazi group distributed hundreds of posters reading "Holocaust Lie of Six Million." In a television discussion about the program, a Nazi sympathizer was invited to express his views, but no Jew was asked to participate.

The anti-Semitism in today's Spain is related to the rise of extremist groups on both the right and the left. The influx into the job market of highly skilled Latin American refugees, some of them Jewish, has only added to the problem. Like the Vatican, the Spanish government has never recognized the state of Israel. Many young Spaniards are "anti-Zionist" and give their support to the Palestine Liberation Organization.

The old views about Jewish financial control and conspiracy also seem to have caught on among many younger writers and journalists. In June 1979, the respected liberal newspaper *El País* published an article suggesting that Spain's small Jewish community might one day become a sinister force in national life: "They are to be found in all places. . . . they control a variety of enterprises but apparently their power isn't dangerous yet."

A few Spaniards have tried to give serious accounts of what happened in Germany and in Spain during the Nazi era, but most Spanish intellectuals have shown little interest in the period. They don't seem to have been alarmed by the growth of anti-Semitism in Spanish life nor to have spoken up in protest.

Argentina

TWO COUNTRIES THAT BEGAN AS European colonies—Argentina and Australia—illustrate the very different shape that anti-Semitism can assume in different areas of the world.

Argentina was the favorite destination of a number of fleeing Nazis, including Adolf Eichmann. It figured prominently in the plans of Nazis hoping to save the movement and themselves. This fit into President Juan Perón's plans to build Argentina's strength by means of a modern army and an independent weapons industry, which the Nazis were to help build. Nazis held key posts in the aircraft industry and in nuclear research institutes, and former German air force pilots acted as advisers to the Argentinian air force. Besides Eichmann himself, a number of his aides found sanctuary in Argentina. The head of the anti-Jewish section of Goebbels's Propaganda Ministry became Perón's adviser. Moreover, the Nazi point of view was carried on by certain German-language publications, like *Der Weg*, published in Buenos Aires. After Perón's fall from power in 1955, some of these fugitives moved on to Egypt, whose own military needs and vicious anti-Semitism provided the Nazis a welcoming atmosphere.

The issue of anti-Semitism in Argentina was most recently discussed by Jacobo Timerman, a Jewish newspaperman. After his flight from that country, he described his experiences in the book *Prisoner Without a Name, Cell Without a Number.* Timerman was editor and publisher of a leading Buenos Aires daily paper when he was arrested by the military government. He was tortured and held without charges for twenty-nine months. Because he was well known, his case attracted attention, and the Jimmy Carter administration, in keeping with its human rights campaign, sought his release. The Supreme Court of Argentina ordered his release twice, but the military continued to hold him. Finally, the generals (who now control Argentina) gave in, but not before they revoked his citizenship, confiscated his newspaper and all his other property, and then expelled him from the country by taking him under guard to a plane bound for Israel. Unlike fifteen thousand other Argentinian citizens who were seized by the military over the previous five years, however, Timerman survived to tell his story.

While he is quick to insist that Jews are not the only ones who suffer in Argentina, he did describe special anti-Semitic torments during his imprisonment. On one occasion he was blindfolded and seated in a chair with his hands tied behind his back. As electric shocks were administered, his unseen torturer shouted a single word, and others present joined in: "Jew! . . . Jew! . . . Jew! . . . Jew!" As they chanted, they clapped their hands and laughed.

According to Timerman, anti-Semitic literature is studied in military academies and sold openly on the streets. The Argentine government considers Zionism more dangerous than even Communism. While in prison, Timerman was interrogated about a secret trip his captors insisted Israeli prime minister Menachem Begin had made to Argentina, and about Zionist plans to seize Patagonia in southern Argentina and to turn it into a second Zionist state.

When Timerman was kidnapped, the first questions he was asked before the military tribunal were always: Are you a Jew? Are you a Zionist? Timerman thinks that his admitting to being a Zionist and having Zionist beliefs may have saved his life, because his interrogators were convinced they had captured a key figure in the world Jewish conspiracy and wanted to save him for a "show trial." Timerman continually refers to the many non-Jewish victims of the military regime, but he also adds: "But in the solitude of prison it is so sad to be beaten for being Jewish. There is such despair when they torture you for being Jewish. It seems so humiliating to have been born."

Amnesty International, a respected human rights organization, confirmed in its report on torture in Argentina that Jews are singled out for especially harsh treatment. During torture, they are interrogated not only about their political ideas, but also about the Jewish community in Argentina. Names and addresses of Jews and diagrams of synagogues and business premises owned by Jews are diligently collected. Some prisoners have even been made to kneel in front of pictures of Hitler and renounce their Jewish heritage.

This special brand of Argentine anti-Semitism, practiced by the military and condoned by the government, is rooted in a repressive attempt to protect the "Christian" social order. One military spokesman told Timerman that Argentina has three main enemies: "Karl Marx, because he tried to destroy the Christian concept of society; Sigmund Freud, because he tried to destroy the Christian concept of the family; and Albert Einstein, because he tried to destroy the Christian concept of time and space." These "enemies" of Argentina happen to have been the three principal architects of the modern world, and all three of them were Jews.

Australia

IN AUSTRALIA, THE PROBLEM OF ANTI-SEMITISM takes quite a different shape. Jews make up only about one half of one percent of Australia's fifteen million people, and most of them live in the two largest cities, Melbourne and Sydney. Jews have lived in Australia since the very first European settlement in 1788, and they have been prominent in Australian society ever since. The commander-in-chief of the Australian army in Europe during World War I was Jewish, as was the first Australian-born Governor General (acting head of state).

Anti-Semitism surfaced there in the 1930s and 1940s with the arrival of refugees from Hitler's Germany. Most of the opposition to this wave of Jewish immigrants came from the political right. The little support and encouragement offered came from the left, especially from the Australian Labor Party government, which had allowed the Jews to come.

However, this situation has since reversed itself. As Jews have become more prosperous, they have tended to become more conservative and have moved politically to the right, partly because of the rise of left-wing anti-Zionism in the 1960s. Anti-Zionism and support for the Palestine Liberation Organization have become rallying cries for young radicals. In the past decade, intense anti-Zionism has found a home in Australian politics—on the socialist left wing of some of the state labor parties, in the leadership of the Australian Union of Students, and in the strident voice of a Melbourne radio station that pours out a steady stream of anti-Zionist propaganda.

When Gough Whitlam was the Labor prime minister between 1972 and 1975, he grew increasingly hostile toward Israel and friendly toward the Arab states. Australia's vote in the United Nations and other international bodies shifted from solid support for Israel to abstention, and even to support for the PLO. Although he was voted out of office in December 1975, left-wing anti-Zionism remains a powerful force in Australian politics.

–14–

The United States

IN SPITE OF THEIR GENERALLY SUCCESSFUL integration into the mainstream of American society, Jews have continued to face discrimination in a number of areas. The same forces that worked to restrict immigration also worked to hinder the advancement of the immigrants and their upwardly mobile children and grandchildren. Today the social anti-Semitism of country clubs, private schools and colleges, executive suites, and other circles of privilege is commonplace.

Some sources of religious and racial hatred are vicious and open. Extremist groups like the revived Ku Klux Klan are active and vocal, and the old religious anti-Semitism seems to be one of the unfortunate by-products of many forms of Christian fervor. Also, in recent years, Arabs have had an increasing influence on American foreign policy. Moreover, political attacks against American Jews and, more specifically, the "Jewish lobby" have become more frequent.

Refugees

IT IS SAD AND IRONIC THAT during World War II, while Hitler was carrying out his "final solution," anti-Semitism was growing in the United States. In the 1930s—during the Depression and against the background of the rise of Nazi Germany—the American public rejected the anti-Semitic appeals of the German-American Bund and of the fiery radio priest Father Charles Coughlin and his organization, called the "Christian Front." However, as the war began, polls indicated a growing distrust and resentment against Jews. More than half of the Americans polled thought that Jews had too much influence in business and government, and a sizable number of people questioned Jewish loyalty to America. A quarter of the people polled saw Jews as less patriotic than others, while a third accused them of avoiding the armed services. These anti-Semitic attitudes continued to rise until the very last year of the war when, with the final victory in sight, wartime tensions began to ease.

All through the 1930s, Congress and the American public resisted the entry of Jewish refugees from Hitler's Germany beyond the established quotas. Despite the pleas of various Jewish groups, church leaders, and liberal voices, immigration restrictions were rigidly upheld. A national poll in 1938 found two-thirds of Americans opposed to admitting refugees, and a year later the figure rose to 83 percent.

President Franklin Delano Roosevelt called an international conference to deal with the problem of what to do with refugees from Germany. The conference (held in 1938 in Evian, France) did little to ease the crisis. Lofty statements of concern for the refugees were made, but no specific rescue or settlement plans ever developed. None of the twenty-nine countries present, including the United States, changed its immigration policy because of the conference.

Despite the vigorous campaigning by liberal and Jewish groups for a relaxation of American quotas, President Roosevelt did not lend his public support to changing immigration policy in order to ease the plight of many European Jews. Even a 1939 bill to rescue twenty thousand refugee children failed to pass Congress. Strong resistance to helping such children developed because it was feared that the beneficiaries of the bill, in the words of the Allied Patriotic Societies, "would be for the most part of the Jewish race."

American inaction continued into the war, and when there was finally some movement to aid Jewish victims, it was too little and too late. In 1943 the United States and Britain held a conference on refugee problems in Bermuda, but it was no more productive than the Evian conference had been five years before. Shocking evidence soon emerged that officials in the State Department were not only indifferent to the plight of European Jews, but they were also deliberately preventing plans to rescue Jews from Hitler. Secretary of the Treasury Henry Morgenthau, Jr., submitted to the president a report on the State Department that was bluntly entitled, "Acquiescence of this Government in the Murder of Jews." President Roosevelt was disturbed enough to remove the responsibility for refugee matters from the State Department and to place it in the hands of a specially created War Refugee Board. Had the board been set up years earlier, it might have saved lives, but by the time it was set up in 1944, the Holocaust was almost over.

Right after the war, the United States did not prove to be any more hospitable to concentration camp survivors and displaced persons. In 1948, however, Congress finally did pass the Displaced Persons Act, which provided for the admission of up to four hundred thousand displaced persons.

Patterns of Discrimination

THE JEWISH COMMUNITY HAS PLAYED an important role in American society, especially in the larger cities and population centers. Yet the protective instincts of an old, established upper class, the prejudices of the general population, and ethnic competition have contributed to the discrimination that Jews have had to face in employment, housing, schools, colleges, universities, and social institutions.

When Americans began to realize that this discrimination was part of a larger problem in American life—the denial of rights to blacks and other minorities—the fight against anti-Semitism became part of the broader struggle for civil rights. This civil-rights battle was taken up at the 1948 Democratic Convention. When the advocacy of civil rights became part of the party platform, it became a factor in the general election. A group of southern Democrats led by South Carolina's Senator Strom Thurmond broke away from the Democratic party in protest, but President Harry Truman surprised many people by gaining reelection anyway.

That same year, the United States Supreme Court gave civil

rights advocates a victory on May 3, when it ruled that state and federal courts could not be used to uphold real estate agreements that limited or restricted the sale or occupancy of houses on the basis of race or religion. It was little more than a victory of principle, however, because restrictive practices were not outlawed as such. In many areas real estate brokers continued to practice the right to discriminate upheld by the code of ethics of the National Association of Real Estate Boards, which stated: "Realtors should never be instrumental in introducing into a neighborhood . . . members of any race or nationality . . . whose presence will be clearly detrimental to property values."

At the beginning of the century, when immigrant eastern Jews first began showing up at universities in and around New York City, schools devised ways to limit their numbers. More than any other group of immigrants, Jews were applying to educational institutions that considered themselves custodians of older American elitist values. Whenever the number of Jewish students grew to the point of making them visible, criticism would surface. They were charged with "lacking polish" and "not fitting in." Just to make sure they didn't fit in, these schools barred Jewish students from fraternities, eating clubs, and honor societies.

At City College of New York in 1913, a national fraternity dropped its local chapter because it had pledged too many Jews. In 1922 New York University suddenly cut down on the number of Jewish students it admitted, to "restore the balance." When Columbia University found its Jewish enrollment in 1920 had risen to 40 percent, it quickly took steps to cut it back to 22 percent within two years.

This attempt to curb the number of young Jews seeking admission to universities came out into the open in 1922 when the president of Harvard University, A. Lawrence Lowell, advised that the university limit the number of Jewish students it admitted. Actually, Harvard was one of the few Ivy League schools that did admit a significant number of Jews. Over the years, the proportion of Jewish students had grown to 20 percent. Lowell wrote to a Jewish alumnus, who had written to protest this proposed change, that it would be to the advantage of Jews if not so many of them came to Harvard.

The bluntness of his remarks spread beyond Harvard and ignited a public debate. The issue had first arisen at Harvard because of the growing anti-Semitism on the part of its students and faculty members. The following year, student and faculty forums discussed the issues openly, which helped reduce the tensions on campus. Finally, the matter was put in the hands of a faculty committee, which concluded that a formal quota system would run counter to the Harvard tradition of "equal opportunity for all, regardless of race and religion." However, the committee did go on to recommend that the university seek a broader geographical representation for its student body. Since the Jewish population was heavily concentrated in certain eastern states, the effect of that policy was to cut the proportion of Jewish students in half by 1931, although that percentage did rise again once Lowell's term as university president was over.

This practice of secret quotas to restrict the number of Jewish students persisted beyond World War II. A B'nai B'rith survey in 1946 found that Jewish students made up about 9 percent of the two million American college students, but 77 percent of these Jews were concentrated in fifty of the largest schools; the better of the small schools were still discriminating against them. A study of Jews in professional schools (7 percent of the student body) showed similar patterns of discrimination.

In 1947 the Jewish Anti-Defamation League gave the American Council on Education a grant to investigate these discriminatory practices. They studied the college admissions figures for the high school class of 1947. This national survey showed that Jewish students had the highest interest (over Protestants and Catholics) in applying to college, but that they were also the most pessimistic about their chances. Their percentage of admission was as high as the others', but they were not accepted as readily by their preferred schools. In the Northeast, where the Jewish population was concentrated, the percentage of first-choice acceptances for Jews was even lower. To counteract this continuing practice of discrimination, Jewish students had to apply to far more schools than did non-Jews. Figures based on the number of applications filed at American colleges and universities were equally revealing: of the total number of Protestant students who applied, 77 percent were accepted; 67 percent of Catholics were accepted; and only 57 percent of Jewish students were accepted.

Medical schools also resorted to secret quotas, often overlooking the merit of individual candidates in a desire to limit the proportion of Jewish students. As a result, the number of Jewish students in the medical schools of New York State in 1920 was cut in half by 1940. Likewise, the proportion of Jews in veterinary medicine dropped from almost 12 percent in 1935 to less than 2 percent in 1946.

At Columbia University's College of Physicians and Surgeons, 40 percent of the medical students had once been Jewish, but after a quota system was adopted, the proportion fell to between 10 and 15 percent by the 1930s. The Cornell Medical School, also in New York City, used the quota system. In 1940 the dean of the school explained that Cornell accepted a class of eighty (out of twelve hundred applicants), ten of whom were Jews. However, because seven hundred of the applicants were Jewish, a Jewish applicant's chance for acceptance was one in seventy, or *ten* times harder than for a non-Jew, whose chance for acceptance was one in seven. Since schools in other states had similar admissions policies and some state universities also put limits on out-of-state students, Jews faced severe discrimination in many important American institutions of higher learning.

Despite progress, discrimination against Jews continued. A study published in 1968 concluded that relatively few Jews were found in executive positions in the banking, insurance, automobile, and shipping industries. At about the same time, a survey of thirty-eight major companies in the New York City area showed that the proportion of Jews to non-Jews in executive positions was relatively small. Private employment agencies tended to perpetuate these patterns of discrimination by catering to the real or imagined prejudices of their clients.

After World War II certain resort hotels continued to exclude Jews. A study in 1956 and 1957 showed that one out of every four American hotels had such practices. Country clubs and city social clubs also continued to discriminate. A 1961 survey revealed that three-quarters of country clubs and well over half the city clubs excluded Jews or maintained quotas against them. And, of course, "exclusive" neighborhoods were just that; they excluded Jews and other minorities by means of restrictive real-estate practices—even though the Supreme Court ruled that such discrimination is illegal.

Jewish employees of corporations often have found it difficult to advance. Discrimination against them at the executive level keeps them from being eligible for certain residential areas and country clubs, while exclusion from such clubs and neighborhoods keeps them from moving to the highest levels of industry, since top-level businessmen who frequent these clubs tend to promote the people they know best.

Arab Pressures

ANTI-ISRAEL PRESSURES FROM ARAB countries have had their effects in the United States on both American business and foreign policy. In conjunction with their economic boycott of Israel, Arabs have put pressure on American businesses that do business in the Arab world to avoid dealing with Israel, or even to refrain from using Jewish employees.

Because of the importance of Arab oil, many American companies have given in to this pressure, at least to some degree. Several have even gone so far as to drop Jewish employees in order to make themselves more attractive to the Arabs. A midwestern medical supply company agreed to prohibit its Jewish employees from handling any part of a goods shipment under a twenty-million-dollar contract with Saudi Arabia. Another company eliminated all identifiably Jewish names from its brochures as part of a sales campaign to attract Arab business. A teacher recruitment agency, when it advertised jobs for Middle Eastern schools, announced that Jews and those with Jewish names should not apply.

From 1975 to 1978, the Anti-Defamation League worked to get legislation through Congress that would end the boycott. The Department of Commerce and a number of American companies had quietly been cooperating with Arab demands, since Arab propagandists and their allies in American business predicted serious economic consequences if Arab "religious sensitivities" were not honored. One such spokesman against the anti-boycott bill, then making its way through Congress, was Spiro Agnew, the former vice president under Richard Nixon. Having become a pro-Arab business consultant after being forced to resign in disgrace from the vice presidency, he warned that opposition to the Arab boycott was the way to "commit hara-kiri to satisfy the small but powerful Zionist lobby."

Despite these pressures, Congress finally did pass legislation that made it illegal to discriminate against Jews or to avoid trading with Israel out of compliance with Arab boycott pressures. At the signing ceremony in the Rose Garden of the White House on June 22, 1978, President Carter said that the bill "seeks to end the divisive effects on American life of a foreign boycott aimed at Jewish members of our society."

Criticism of the "Israel lobby" has since been voiced at the highest levels of government—both in the halls of Congress and in the corridors of the executive branch. American foreign policy has recently become more "balanced" by tilting toward "moderate" Arab states, and the Administration has pushed for the sale of F-15 fighter bombers and AWACS reconnaissance planes to Saudi Arabia. Opposition to such sales has been blamed on the "Jewish lobby," or, in Agnew's words, "the small but powerful Zionist lobby."

In the intense debate over the AWACS sale on the Senate floor in October 1981, thinly-disguised anti-Semitic charges were directed at American Jews who opposed the sale. They were pictured as the main obstacle, putting the interests of a foreign nation (Israel) ahead of the American national interest. Senator Steven Symms of Idaho said, "The perception is that there's been undue pressure from the American Jewish community."

President Ronald Reagan blamed "foreign" sources for the opposition, announcing on national evening news broadcasts that "It is not the business of other nations to make American foreign policy." As it turned out, the Administration gained the Senate approval it needed for the sale, and the passions raised by the debate died down. Nonetheless, the issue did reveal the emergence of anti-Semitic undercurrents when the issue of support for Israel is at stake.

The Latent Danger

ANTI-SEMITISM CONTINUES TO FIND open and violent expression among such extremist groups as the American Nazis and the Ku Klux Klan. The openness of their hatred can be shocking. An Alabama Klan leader was quoted not long ago in a national magazine as saying, "The Jewish problem must be settled, a Final Solution. I am not going to hang up my robe until the last Jew is deported to Palestine or executed."

Other groups on the Radical Right, such as the John Birch Society and the Liberty Lobby, have also been active agents of anti-Semitism. On the Radical Left, too, the anti-Zionist propaganda of groups like the Socialist Workers' Party spills over into anti-Semitic attacks on Jews in America. The Black Panthers, active during the 1960s, were openly anti-Semitic as a result of their close identification with the Third World and its anti-Zionism. The Black Muslims have also adopted the zealous anti-Zionism of the Islamic world.

In a number of black ghettos, anti-Semitic resentments linger on because Jews were often the last immigrant occupants of the neighborhoods into which blacks moved. In New York's Harlem, for example, many store owners and landlords were Jewish at the time blacks moved in. Hence, black frustrations against the "system" or the "white power structure" would often be directed against Jews. In New York City the high proportion of Jewish administrators and teachers in the public school system caused a black-Jewish confrontation in the 1970s over the issue of school decentralization and neighborhood control. The heated debate sometimes boiled over into openly expressed prejudices on both sides of the argument.

In the struggle for civil rights and for an end to discrimination in American life, Jews and blacks have been natural allies, but in recent years there have been signs of a strain in the coalition as the civil rights movement has receded and the foreign policy issue of support for Israel has taken center stage.

In many other parts of the country, Jews are perceived as active supporters of civil rights, racial integration, and various liberal causes, and they are resented by conservatives for that very reason. This criticism of Jews from different directions brings to mind how nineteenth-century European Jews were attacked from both sides— from the left for being wealthy capitalists, and from the right for being revolutionary Marxists.

In the 1960s, the Anti-Defamation League sponsored a major study to assess the degree of anti-Semitism in the general public. The Survey Research Center of the University of California at

Berkeley conducted the study and found that anti-Semitic attitudes were widespread. Some of the attitudes were subtle, based more on stereotypes than on direct contact with Jewish people. However, the study did find that a large part of the sampling—over a third—were highly anti-Semitic. They believed that Jews had negative traits; they were perceived as too powerful, aggressive, proud, clannish, or unethical. More than 25 percent of the survey defended the right of social clubs to exclude Jews, while another 29 percent, who were against the idea, nonetheless wouldn't do anything to oppose the practice.

In fact, perhaps the most disturbing finding of the study was the widespread indifference to social and political discrimination on the part of the less prejudiced part of the population. This apathetic majority had no firm position on bigotry, or no principled commitment to democratic values. Although only 5 percent of the sample would actively seek out anti-Semitic candidates to vote for, fully a third of them indicated that if a candidate were anti-Semitic, it would make no difference to them. Indeed, those in the survey who turned out to be "principled and consistent opponents of anti-Semitism" were a small minority (16 percent).

The indications from this study are that if the political pendulum should swing in the direction of open anti-Semitism at some future time of crisis or unrest, there is an apathetic majority who might simply follow the drift of the times. Those who would raise their voices in protest or actively oppose the trend would be in a distinct minority. Much American Jewish support for Israel comes from those who strongly feel that only there will Jews be safe from outbreaks of anti-Semitism.

There are also signs that in certain areas of American life, anti-Semitic voices are growing bolder. In 1980 the Reverend Bailey Smith, president of the Southern Baptist Convention with its 13.5 million members, declared publicly that "Almighty God does not hear the prayer of the Jew." Several weeks later, his point of view was reinforced by the Reverend Jerry Falwell (the leader of the Moral Majority), who said, "I believe God does not hear the prayers of unredeemed gentiles or Jews."

There are such voices in the political arena as well. In California not long ago, State Senator John Schmitz called the opponents of his bill to restrict abortion "lesbians" and "murderous marauders."

He described what he saw when he looked out at the audience of the hearing as "a sea of hard, Jewish and arguably female faces." Afterwards, he refused to amend his statements and accused his critics of being dominated by Jews. The State Senate Rules Committee stripped him of a committee chairmanship and fired him from a commission on women in the wake of the controversy, but that did not deter Schmitz from his quest for the Republican nomination for the United States Senate, which he failed to win.

The 1980 election also affirmed the political potential for anti-Semitism. In Michigan a self-proclaimed Nazi and racist ran for Congress (in the Fifteenth Congressional District). Not only did he secure the Republican nomination, but he also won 53,570 votes in the general election—one third of the total number of votes.

Political anti-Semitism may have a potential that has been generally underestimated, and perhaps it is waiting for more troubled times to show itself. Senator Mark Hatfield of Oregon sees just such a possibility. He is chairman of the Senate Appropriations Committee, and in 1981 he was an opponent of the Administration's sale of the AWACS planes to Saudi Arabia. On the basis of the debate, the mail that came into his office, and his conversations with residents of his state, he concluded that there was a great deal of "latent anti-Semitism" in the country that is "just waiting for a trigger mechanism to set it off."

There is little evidence that in the future the United States will prove to be any more resistant to anti-Semitism than Europe was. The same Constitution that provides American Jewish citizens full and equal protection under the law also provides freedom of speech and expression to the voices of anti-Semitism, racism, and other forms of prejudice. Since attitudes cannot be legislated out of existence, it is certain that the voices of hatred will continue to be heard. Should the years ahead grow more tense and troubled, those voices are destined to become louder.

Conclusion

AFTER LOOKING AT THE EVIDENCE of history, one is tempted to conclude that anti-Semitism is inevitable; that as long as there is Judaism and a Jewish people maintaining its separate identity and traditions, there will always be anti-Semitism. If the horrors of the Holocaust were not able to defeat and shame out of existence the legacy of anti-Semitism, what will it take?

Yet the prospects aren't all bleak. There have been scattered signs of hope. Christianity, the source of so much anti-Semitism in the past, seems to be more aware of the responsibility it bears. Christian churches have yet to take action to modify the negative picture of Jews and Judaism that is found in the New Testament, but some have taken more modest steps.

At meetings in Amsterdam in 1948 and New Delhi in 1961, the predominantly Protestant World Council of Churches condemned anti-Semitism and expressed regret for not having acted more decisively during the Nazi years. On the Catholic side, an important change of attitude took place during the reign of Pope John XXIII. The Catholics removed anti-Jewish references from the Good Friday liturgy that they had been reciting for centuries. In 1965, at the Second Vatican Council, the Catholic Church declared that it no longer held the Jewish people responsible for the death of Christ. Also, many Christian groups have taken steps to remove anti-Jewish statements from their textbooks.

Nevertheless, a number of Christian churches, both Catholic and Protestant, remain lukewarm—or even hostile—to the state of

Israel. The Vatican has yet to extend diplomatic recognition to Israel, and the pope continues to ask that Jerusalem be under international rather than Jewish control. There are also signs that Christian churches, having taken up the cause of the Palestinians, are increasingly receptive to anti-Israel propaganda, some of which emanates from churches in the Arab world.

With regard to Israel's future, there is reason for both concern and hope. The original Zionist dream was that the creation of a Jewish state would eliminate anti-Semitism, since Jews would no longer need to live as vulnerable aliens in other peoples' countries. However, Israel has lived under seige from the day of its birth, surrounded by a hostile Arab world.

If and when the day arrives when the Palestinian conflict is resolved and Israel is allowed to live in peace with its Arab neighbors, then Arab anti-Semitism will surely decline. Already the peace treaty between Egypt and Israel has reduced considerably the anti-Israel rhetoric that once poured forth from Cairo.

Whatever the shape of anti-Semitism in the future, it will have to contend—as it always has—with the indomitable spirit of the Jewish people. The story of discrimination, persecution, and mass murder that Jews have had to endure, and that this book has sought to detail, should not obscure the fact that the Jewish people have survived and prevailed. Max Dimont has described the Jews as "indestructible," and no other people has proved to be as durable and as resilient. No other people has survived from ancient times, preserving to such a degree its beliefs, values, and traditions, while contributing so much to civilization along the way.

Finally, it needs to be said that Jews were not the only victims of Hitler and the Nazis, so the story of anti-Semitism and the Holocaust can never remain just a matter for Jewish history. It is a story that belongs to all of mankind. To keep the human race from forgetting this horror, over six thousand survivors of Nazi death camps met in Jerusalem in June 1981 for the World Gathering of Jewish Holocaust Survivors. They came from twenty-three countries to bear witness to that event, the lessons of which the world will ignore only at its own great peril.

These survivors are now dying out, so at the closing ceremony about a thousand of the sons and daughters of the survivors—the

Second Generation—made a solemn pledge to keep alive the remembrance of the Holocaust for future generations.

The world sorely needs to remember that injustice to one is injustice to all, that injustice visited on a single people, or even a single person, never stops there. Anti-Semitism, a disease that will spread if not checked, is ultimately dangerous to everyone. Many have had to learn this lesson the hard way. One of them was a German pastor, Martin Niemöller, who was arrested in 1938 and spent the war in a concentration camp:

> *First the Nazis went after the Jews, but I wasn't a Jew, so I did not react. Then they went after the Catholics, but I wasn't a Catholic, so I didn't object. Then they went after the worker, but I wasn't a worker, so I didn't stand up. Then they went after the Protestant clergy, but by then it was too late for anybody to stand up.*

Samuel Pisar, a survivor of Auschwitz who was in Jerusalem for the gathering, put it even more simply. "It begins with the Jews," he said, "but it becomes an assault on everyone."

Suggested Reading

Ainsztein, Reuben, *The Warsaw Ghetto Revolt*, N.Y., Holocaust Library (distributed by Schocken), 1979.

Belth, Nathan, *A Promise To Keep: A Narrative of the American Encounter with Anti-Semitism*, N.Y., Schocken, 1981.

Craig, Gordon, *Germany, 1866–1945*, N.Y., Oxford University Press, 1978.

Dawidowicz, Lucy, *The War Against the Jews, 1933–1945*, N.Y., Holt, Rinehart and Winston, 1975.

Des Pres, Terrence, *The Survivor: An Anatomy of Life in the Death Camps*, N.Y., Pocket, 1977.

Dimont, Max, *Jews, God and History*, N.Y., Signet, 1962.

Elkins, Michael, *Forged in Fury*, N.Y., Ballantine, 1971.

Flannery, Edward, *The Anguish of the Jews*, N.Y., Macmillan, 1965.

Frank, Anne, *The Diary of a Young Girl*, N.Y., Pocket, 1953.

Katz, Jacob, *Out of the Ghetto: The Social Background of Jewish Emancipation, 1770–1870*, N.Y., Schocken, 1978.

Levi, Primo, *Survival in Auschwitz*, N.Y., Collier, 1961.

Meltzer, Milton, *Never To Forget: The Jews of the Holocaust*, N.Y., Dell, 1977.

Poliakov, Leon, *Harvest of Hate: The Nazi Program for the Destruction of the Jews of Europe*, N.Y., Holocaust Library (distributed by Schocken), 1979.

———, *The History of Anti-Semitism*, N.Y., Schocken, 1974.

Shirer, William, *The Rise and Fall of the Third Reich*, N.Y., Fawcett, 1978.

Suhl, Yuri, *They Fought Back: The Story of Jewish Resistance in Nazi Europe,* N.Y., Schocken, 1975.

Taylor, A.J.P., *The Course of German History,* N.Y., Capricorn, 1962.

———, *The Second World War,* N.Y., Berkley, 1978.

Timerman, Jacobo, *Prisoner Without a Name, Cell Without a Number,* N.Y., Vintage, 1982.

Wiesel, Elie, *Night,* N.Y., Avon, 1972.

Index

Russian Revolution, 42, 55, 64, 110
Russification, 39

S.A. *(Sturmabteilung)*, 63, 68, 74
Sachsenhausen, 75, 100
St. Louis, 78
"Salon Jews," 22
Saudi Arabia, 108, 132, 136
Schmeling, Max, 71
Schmitz, John, 135–36
Seligman, Joseph, 45
Seneca, 6
Sephardic Jews, 43
"Show trials," 113, 115, 124
Shtetls, 37, 80
Simmons, William, 50–51
Six-Day War, 108, 116, 120
Slánský, Rudolf, 115
Slaton, Governor John, 49
"Slavophilism," 39
Smith, the Reverend Bailey, 135
Sobibor, 93, 101
Social Democrats, 61, 67
Socialism, 26–27; Jewish, 30, 111
Socialist Workers' Party, 134
Solidarity, 118
Sonderkommando, 99, 102
Southern Baptist Convention, 135
Soviet Union, 42, 72, 80, 83, 88–91, 93, 105–6, 110–17. *See also* Russia, czarist
Spain, 14, 72, 121–22
Spanish Inquisition, 14–15, 43, 121
Spinoza, Baruch, 22
S.S. *(Schutzstaffel),* 68, 73–74, 76–77, 82, 86, 89, 93–94, 96–97, 99, 100–102, 120
Stalin, Joseph, 114–15
Sterilization, of Jews, 87, 101

Stöcker, Adolf, 30
Streicher, Julius, 64, 65
Stürmer, Der, 64
Sturma, 78
Stuyvesant, Peter, 43
Sudetenland, 73
Suez Canal, 106
Survey Research Center, 134–35
Symms, Senator Steven, 133
Syria, 106, 108

Tacitus, 6
Taft, William Howard, 52
Tall, Abdallah al-, 107
Talmud, 14, 17
Talmud Jew, The (Rohling), 29, 32
Talmud Torahs, 113
Thadden, Adolf von, 119
Theresienstadt, 96
Third World, 109
Thurmond, Strom, 128
Timerman, Jacobo, 123–24
Torquemada, Tomás de, 14
Treblinka, 83, 93–94, 96, 101
Treitschke, Heinrich von, 30
Trotsky, Leon, 111
Truman, Harry, 128
Turkey, 15, 35, 78
Twain, Mark, 45

Uganda, 35
Ukraine, the, 15, 55, 89, 115
Union Générale, 32
United Nations, 105–6, 109, 125
United States, 40, 42–52, 68, 78, 80, 88, 105–6, 116, 126–36
Urban II, Pope, 11
Uris, Leon, 121

Vatican, 122, 137
Versailles Treaty, 71, 81
Vichy, 86, 97, 120
Victory of Judaism over Germanism, The (Marr), 29